Praise for Second Shelter

"Haid and Donnelly have provided an invaluable resource for parents facing the daunting decision to enroll their child in a therapeutic program. Packed full of practical education and expert guidance, you'll feel as if these two are holding your hand, anticipating your questions, and reassuring you through their combined personal and professional experience."   —Paul Case, Psy.D., author of *What Now? How Teen Theraputic Programs Could Save Your Troubled Child*

"*Second Shelter* is truly a must read for all parents whose children are struggling and may be in need of a therapeutic boarding school. It is an extraordinary book—well researched, skillfully presented, and beautifully written. From this book you will gain insight and information, and, perhaps as importantly, you will know that you are not alone."
                         —Ronald J. Greer, Minister and Director of Pastoral
                    Counseling at Peachtree Road United Methodist Church,
                    Atlanta, and author of *Now That They Are Grown*

"A lovely fusion of information and intimate conversation about the authors' odyssey to find appropriate emotional treatment for their adolescents. The beauty in this story can be found in its deep personalization of its characters, their grief and sorrow, their joy and faith. This book would be a welcome gift to both mental health professionals and parents in similar circumstances."
                              —Ray J. Kuckleburg, Ph.D., Psychotherapist

"A much needed, helpful guide. Haid and Donnelly's advice to parents on how to partner with the school to achieve the best outcome, how to handle home visits, and how to deal with predictable regressions and the emotional roller coaster of all the family members is invaluable. Second Shelter *is a comprehensive, essential manual for parents who seek to find that 'shelter' where the dysfunctional teen can transform into an adolescent who can once again function at home and at school."*
 —Dr. Martha Burdette, Ben Franklin Academy, Atlanta, Georgia

SECOND SHELTER

Family Strategies for Navigating
Therapeutic Boarding Schools and
Residential Treatment Centers

Rebecca Haid, MEd
and Elizabeth W. Donnelly, MS

LANTERN BOOKS / NEW YORK
A Division of Booklight Inc.

2013
Lantern Books
128 Second Place
Brooklyn, NY 11231
www.lanternbooks.com

Printed in the United States of America

Cover photo by Sam Haid.

Library of Congress Cataloging-in-Publication information available.

ISBN: 9781590563984

For Reg and Sam
And for those we've lost

—REBECCA HAID

For Emmeline

—ELIZABETH DONNELLY

CONTENTS

INTRODUCTION

A PARENT'S EXPERIENCE
(REBECCA HAID)

"I'd recommend you enroll Andy in a therapeutic program or some sort of emotional-growth school at this point. I can't see sending him back to a regular day-school environment given everything that has happened. I've got the names of a couple of good educational consultants here in town who should be able to help you find the right place for him. And I'd act on this as soon as you can; I wouldn't delay making the decision."

Shock. Shock is a pretty accurate description of what my husband and I felt when my stepson Andy's psychiatrist talked to us after meeting with him for several therapy sessions and going through all his test results. I felt like I'd been tossed against a wall by a bomb blast. Yes, of course we knew Andy had struggled with depression and that his grades were falling. Yes, we knew he had become more isolated from us and from his peers over the last few months, and we knew he was spending too much time on the Internet and on Facebook. We knew he was still trying to cope with the aftermath of his parents' divorce, his mom's recovery from alcoholism, and all the pressures of middle school. What we didn't realize was how deep and pervasive

Andy's problems had become or how quickly they had overrun his ability to cope with school and with his peers on a day-to-day basis. I'd thought Andy's psychiatrist might change his medications or recommend a more intensive counseling schedule, but to send Andy away from home? That was unthinkable . . . or was it?

Andy's world was disintegrating so quickly we knew we had to take immediate action or we might lose him. In a little more than six months, we went from packing up the lights and lanterns from Andy's fourteenth birthday party (where all his classmates hoisted him on their shoulders and sang to him) to packing up his luggage for the two-thousand-mile trip to a tiny school in a remote corner of northern Montana. What in the world had happened to this adorable, loveable kid, and how had things gotten so out of hand this quickly?

I could try to tell you Andy's whole story, but it is not my story to tell. One day Andy may write his own story, and if he does, he will write it with more honesty and poignancy than I could ever muster. And in the end, only Andy knows what really happened. As a stepparent, I knew that Andy was an actor, a comedian, a singer. He was much more interested in the creative process than in the classroom experience, and his grades, even at their best, reflected his perspective. But on the creative side, Andy excelled. He had auditioned and been accepted to the summer theater camp at Interlochen Center for the Arts, and he had animated a ghost story cartoon with the software program we gave him for Christmas. His video parodies of different members of our extended family were acerbic and hysterically funny, and even though he had only taken a few months of piano lessons, he was already picking out the chord progressions from Coldplay songs. Andy had talent; Andy had imagination; Andy had a hilarious, self-effacing sense of humor that smoothed over even the acrimonious family conflicts. It was impossible for me to stay angry with this kid for more than five minutes. He was so endearing, so funny, so charming . . . and therein lay part of the problem. Andy was also a con man. He fooled us all—even some of the most experienced and knowledgeable counselors in Atlanta. But he didn't fool his psychiatrist; she pegged him almost immediately.

As a stepparent, I hoped I would be able to stay impartial and have a clearer, more unbiased perspective about Andy's strengths and weaknesses than his biological mom and dad had. I hoped I could stay somewhat disengaged emotionally and help him make better decisions about his academics and his excessive computer time. It was a naïve hope. I got swept up in the conflict along with everyone else in the family.

It would be too easy to blame all of Andy's problems on the corrosive pop culture mantra of "everything you want, whenever you want it," but that mindset did play a significant part in his struggle. Andy was a privileged kid materially, and the atmosphere of the affluent private school he attended reinforced that mantra nearly every day. We could also pin some of the blame on the bullying Andy endured over social networking, texts, and from the negative comments that were made about his YouTube videos. In trying to give Andy the electronic tools and access he wanted and thought he needed for creative work, we also opened a portal for Andy's exploitation (and the double entendre of that statement is intentional).

Andy's own neurological and psychological hardwiring was also an element in his troubles. Genetically, he was at risk for developing serious emotional problems. And finally, and perhaps most importantly, Andy's biological parents and I were a source of his problems. His parents' divorce, the difference in their parenting and discipline styles, and the sudden imposition of a stepmother's more rigid social, religious, and academic standards into Andy's daily routine created even more confusion and frustration for him. The stress factors piled up on Andy day after day, and the conditions that led to his emotional unraveling are all too common throughout the country. No doubt some, if not all, of these factors are impacting your own children, students, or clients.

As serious as Andy's problems were, he was seldom openly defiant toward us, he was never violent, and, to the best of our knowledge, he was not experimenting with drugs . . . at least not yet. My husband and I caught him early. Andy admitted he was floundering. He knew he needed help. We started the search for a therapeutic school as a collaborative effort with Andy himself, our exceptional educational consultant, and Andy's teachers and physician. We didn't have to send Andy off kicking and screaming to a wilderness program with an escort team (those programs and services will be discussed in depth in chapter 6), nor did we have to go through a harrowing drug or alcohol detox program before he started his therapeutic work. We know how lucky we were on that score.

Looking for a therapeutic or emotional-growth boarding school for Andy became a skewed version of what looking at colleges had been with our older children. After reviewing all the psychological and cognitive testing on Andy (and we had years' worth of it), our educational consultant drew up a list of schools she thought would be a good fit for him. After reading and doing online research about the different schools, we narrowed our choice to two programs that we visited and toured. The staff and student tour guides at both schools told us how rare it was to have a potential student like Andy see the school before he was enrolled, and they remarked that it was almost unheard of for the student to have any voice in selecting the program that his parents ultimately chose. Almost all of the adolescents in both schools had been through wilderness experiential outdoor programs before they started in the residential facilities we toured, but that preliminary work wasn't recommended for Andy.

After less than a few hours on each campus, the choice was clear. The school we visited in New England looked dirty and the boys seemed unkempt and miserable. The food was terrible, and the academic staff didn't have much, if any, flexibility in terms of college preparatory course offerings or independent study. My husband and I commented under our breath that the place reminded us of a Dickens workhouse. We couldn't get away fast enough. Yet, this school had, and still has, an exceptional reputation for the therapeutic work they do with adolescent boys. The school we chose in the northwest corner of Montana was a world away geographically and therapeutically. The campus buildings and grounds were immaculate, and the students were so healthy-looking, friendly, and welcoming that we wondered at first why in the world kids like this were in an emotional-growth school to begin with. The school had a fine arts curriculum in place that was a great fit for Andy's interests, and each of the students was required to take a fine art elective nearly every academic period that they were enrolled. The staff and the teachers seemed as healthy and robust as the children they cared for. Andy didn't want to leave home, but he *wanted* to go to this school in Montana.

While Andy was back at home going through so much pain and trouble, his younger sister, Sarah, had started petitioning us nearly every day to let her go away to a traditional boarding school. Who could blame her? She had suffered the bullying and all the cruel middle school fallout from the struggles of her older brother, who was a grade ahead of her. She was caught in the crossfire between him and the constant teasing of their peers. She was also stuck in the middle of the constant friction between her mom and dad and their anxiety about Andy. She wanted to get out of the "noise," and on the surface her transfer to a traditional boarding school made sense. Her grades were excellent, she made good choices overall with her peer group, and she was determined when it came to standing up for herself and expressing her opinions. My husband and I wanted to believe that Sarah was okay, although we had clear warning signs that she was in trouble too. Sadly, after less than six months at her new school, Sarah had to be hospitalized, and we had to find a therapeutic program for her as well.

My involvement with therapeutic schools has been one of the most challenging and difficult experiences of my life because, as every parent knows, there is no worry in the world as profound as the worry for one's children. Yet, in spite of all the uncertainty and anxiety my husband and I experienced, we also felt extremely fortunate in our journey. All along the way, we have had phenomenal support from our educational consultant, Andy's psychiatrist, and the educators and therapists at the schools my stepchildren attended. If it had not been for the professionalism and genuine concern of these teachers and health care providers, I honestly don't know where we would be right now . . . or more critically, where our children would be.

The more I read and researched, the more I talked with other parents who faced these same circumstances, the more I realized how little comprehensive, easily accessible information is available not only for the parents of struggling teenagers, but also for many of the school counselors and community-based clinicians who are trying to help families address questions about whether therapeutic schools are a reasonable option for their children, and if they are, how they can go about finding the programs best suited for their children's needs. When Wikipedia is the primary information source you have to answer these kinds of questions, you know you're in trouble. Conflicting information and outright misinformation abounds on the Internet about how emotional-growth boarding schools operate and how effective they are. My family had so many questions: Were we doing the right thing by sending our children away? How much would the treatment cost, and how long would it take? Would the programs work at all? We had no idea what to expect; we had no idea what we were getting ourselves into. And as often as not, *we didn't even know the right questions to ask.*

The goal of this book is to make sure that you and your family are better prepared and better informed than we were in the journey that is ahead of you. In 2005, nearly twenty thousand teenagers were enrolled in private therapeutic school programs across the United States, and if we add the number of adolescents in public sector programs and the juvenile corrections system, plus those children who have fallen through the safety nets and are living on the streets, the numbers of teenagers and young adults who are in need of the counseling and other mental health services that therapeutic schools provide grow into the hundreds of thousands.[1] The need for therapeutic boarding schools and residential treatment centers for teenagers is not an isolated problem that affects only a handful of families anymore. The number of struggling adolescents is growing, and the need for solid, reliable information about the industry that provides therapeutic alternatives for our children is growing right along with it.

A PROFESSIONAL'S INSIGHT (ELIZABETH DONNELLY)

My story is not unlike Rebecca Haid's. I, too, am the parent of two children who had special needs during the storm and stress of adolescence. I have lain awake at night wondering what I did wrong as a parent—questioning what I should have done differently and would it have made any significant difference. More than anything, I was terrified about the uncertainty of the future; what was the next step? After struggling for years to find the right fit academically and socially for my son, who has attention deficit hyperactivity disorder (ADHD), and for my daughter, who has nonverbal learning disorder (NLD), I sought the help of an independent educational consultant. Her advice was invaluable, and for a time the choices we made regarding my children brought some peace of mind and hope to our family. Both children were happy and doing well in school, my son at a traditional boarding school and my daughter at a small girls' school in Atlanta. During this time of relative calm, I began to think seriously about the direction my life was taking and considering what I wanted and needed to do as my children moved on to the next stage in their lives. My decision to become an educational consultant was very intentional and based largely on my personal experiences that provided me insight into the struggles many families face with the education of their children. After being a stay-at-home mom for fifteen years, I returned to graduate school to study educational psychology and build a solid foundation on which to begin my career as an educational consultant.

The research I conducted while I was in graduate school on reading comprehension at underperforming inner-city middle schools only underscored my desire to work with at-risk and struggling adolescents. Over the years, I have developed deep bonds with many of my young friends as I sought to be a mentor with a sympathetic ear for them. Whether as a parent of learning-disabled children, an academician searching for solutions to illiteracy, or a clinician guiding other parents through a crisis with their own families, I'm resolved to serve others in everything that I do.

As a parent, my goal has been to ensure that my children remain happy and healthy while gaining the skills they need to achieve academic success, moving them forward to adulthood as productive members of our society. As an educational consultant, my goal is much the same—to provide my clients the information and support they need to find the educational setting that best fits each student's emotional, social, and academic needs.

Throughout this book we seek to blend our voices, as parents and as educators, to help your family navigate the field of therapeutic boarding schools, residential treatment facilities, and wilderness programs. We want to show you the compassion and empathy you'll need as you begin this journey with your family—we know; we've lived it. While we have collaborated fully in nearly every chapter of this book, there are sections which are focused on a parent's perspective and others which are written from an educational consultant's point of view. To add clarity and ease of reading, we've concluded the passages with our respective initials.

We know that if you're reading this book, your family or people you care about are going through an extraordinary trial too. Our goal in the following chapters is to provide parents and educators the clearest, most accurate information we can about the different types of programs that are available for struggling adolescents. We want to guide you toward a strong educational consultant to help you navigate the search to find the most effective school for your child, and we want to give you a best-odds strategy for finding an appropriate school in the rare situations where there is not a qualified educational consultant available to help you. Finally, we want to give you the information and resources you'll need to prepare practically, emotionally, and financially for the journey your entire family is about to make. The decision to send a son or daughter away for treatment is one of the toughest, most heartbreaking choices a parent can make. Nothing is going to make this process easy, but if you are making decisions armed with valid and reliable information, you'll have some peace of mind knowing that you are doing absolutely everything you can for your child given the circumstances. We want you to begin this process in an enlightened and realistic posture about what these programs can and cannot do for your child, and the challenges you're likely to encounter along the way.

One of the most important things to remember is that you are not alone. The problems and the severity of the problems that necessitate the work of emotional-growth and therapeutic schools are common and growing. Most reputable therapeutic programs have strong parent support groups in place, and if you look closely, you're almost certain to find that someone in your neighborhood, your workplace, or your child's school is going through the same ordeal.

Arming yourself with the information you'll need to make the best decisions with your family about therapeutic schools can feel like coping with an avalanche of data at times. To make the fact gathering less stressful, we've broken out the chapters in such a way that you can get to the data you need without having to read the entire text at once. Access the material you need first and later you can go back and fill in gaps you might have in your information arsenal. We'll begin with the most critical question of all—whether a therapeutic boarding school or residential treatment facility should be a consideration for your child in the first place.

chapter 1

The Toughest Decision: Determining Whether a Therapeutic Boarding School Is Appropriate for Your Child

It started with the flu. Andy got sick the week after school started after Christmas break. He missed over a week of classes, and when he was finally able to go back, he was weak physically and behind academically. His classroom teacher was wonderful. She gave Andy modified assignments and plenty of time to make up the work. But Andy was overwhelmed . . . he couldn't or wouldn't do the work. He lied to us about completing assignments and showed us the first couple of pages of reports and projects that were supposedly finished. He substituted old work for new assignments. Obviously, the eighth-grade teaching team caught the ruse immediately, but they gave Andy one more chance. He lied again about completing his work, and he began hiding out from classes, slipping into empty classrooms or the library to avoid his teachers. He would hide in the gym or the counselor's office to avoid going to physical education classes. He couldn't make it through the day at school anymore. We got several calls at midday to pick him up from the counselor's office where we'd find him shaking and crying.

Not surprisingly, we got a letter and a phone call from the middle school principal and the headmaster about a week after this behavior started. Andy's actions had become too disruptive for the other students in his classroom and too much for the eighth-grade teaching team to manage. They told us compassionately but frankly that until Andy could function more effectively and make it through the normal school schedule, he needed to withdraw from school. Andy had already had two sessions with his psychiatrist at this point, and clearly it was time to go back for more help. —R. H.

NO PARENT COMES to the crossroads of a decision to send a son or daughter away from home for psychological treatment or special education without experiencing pain, guilt, and round after round of second-guessing. How many sleepless nights does any family endure before they come to the conclusion that they can't take care of their child's needs at home any longer? Circumstances have to be extreme, without any realistic hope that the situation is going to improve unless significant changes are made. The thought of sending a child away is unthinkable. It's the anathema to what every parent wants to do; yet sometimes it is the only viable choice. Throughout this book and in conversations with your children and their counselors, you'll read and hear the phrase "sending your child away" repeatedly. The phrase has such a negative connotation that most parents wince whenever they hear it. We wince as well; however, that's the way using a therapeutic school to help adolescents is commonly described by parents, educators, and students alike.

Psychologists and educators don't have a set formula or decision-making protocol when it comes to determining which children will be best served in a therapeutic boarding school environment. Instead, clinicians tend to look at clusters of characteristics in the child's behavior and factors in the child's environment before they make this difficult recommendation to parents. Understanding the factors professionals consider as they make the recommendation for a therapeutic placement can often help parents accept the referral as warranted. No parent wants to hear this recommendation, obviously, but seeing the rationale makes it a little easier.

First, if a student's educational, developmental, and/or emotional needs cannot be met in a traditional day-school or boarding school environment, then some type of residential placement which can address those needs may be warranted. In many instances, community-based therapeutic programs or local alternative schools will be a better choice for families, but often, complex emotional or learning needs can't be adequately addressed even with an Individualized Education Program (IEP) or a 504 Plan in a city or county's public school system.

Individualized Education Programs—IEPs, as they are commonly known—are formal written plans and program strategies that describe the educational goals for students who meet the federal requirements for special education. The IEP not only prescribes goals but also outlines the methods by which students will try to meet those goals. Every student who qualifies for an IEP has a document which is tailored for his or her unique needs, and the plan is updated on a regular basis until the student has graduated from high school or until he or she reaches the age of twenty-two. Writing an IEP is the collaborative effort between parents, teachers, a representative of the child's school district, as well as other educational professionals (such as counselors or speech therapists, for example) who are directly involved with the student's work.

Section 504 Plans are set up a bit differently. These written educational plans were developed for compliance with the Federal Rehabilitation Act of 1973 and are designed to provide enhanced access to educational environments for disabled students in elementary school through high school. 504 Plans provide for physical accommodations such as wheelchair access as well as provisions for materials such as large-print textbooks or extended time on assignments or tests. Students who do not qualify for an IEP may receive the assistance they need through a 504 Plan.

If the child's problems are primarily psychological in nature and if different counseling models have been ineffective even when therapeutic work has been frequent and focused, then it may be time to consider an emotional-growth school or a residential treatment facility. It goes without saying that most families are going to exhaust all local therapeutic programs and different treatment approaches before they cross the threshold and consider enrolling their children in a school away from home.

Parents have to be realistic, too, about what's going on under the family roof when they make the decision to send an adolescent away. If the child's mental health or substance abuse issues are too acute or disruptive to the family's overall functioning, or if the child is presenting a safety risk to other family members or himself, parents may have no choice but to move their child into an outdoor therapeutic program (these experiential programs are often called "wilderness" or "wilderness therapy," and we'll discuss them in depth in chapter 3) or directly into a treatment facility. And unfortunately, there are occasions when the family situation itself is too unhealthy or unstable for the teenager to have a reasonable chance of making any progress in working through his or her own therapeutic issues. In those circumstances, too, an alternative educational setting away from home may be the best or only option.

Yet, how do families know when they've finally reached the point where they need to seriously consider a residential program? After all, every teenager goes through tremendous struggle and growth during adolescence. Adolescents are much like toddlers in the rate and complexity of change they're facing physically, cognitively, and emotionally. Adolescence is by definition a time of great upheaval and stress. What makes one struggling teenager a candidate for a residential program when another child with similar problems would be better served at home? The answer seems to lie in the severity of the problems, the duration of the problems, whether the issues are showing any consistent signs of improvement, and whether the problems have been resistant to several different traditional therapeutic approaches. If the troubles are significant, if they've been going on for months and months without any sign of improvement, and if routine counseling isn't helping, it's time to consider a therapeutic school.

Dr. Paul Case, a psychologist with years of experience in both wilderness and therapeutic schools, addresses the problems of adolescents who haven't been adequately helped by the traditional counseling approaches in community-based therapy. In advocating for residential programs, he writes, "Adolescents are good at snowing their therapists. One-hour-per-week sessions can create comfort and rapport between the therapist and his teenaged client, but it is often not enough to create the kind of relationship and involvement that will produce the maturity and change that we are hoping for. . . . Likewise, I believe that adolescents are often too influenced by their peers to really benefit from one-on-one counseling. Teenagers may mean what they say to a therapist in a session, but to apply their insights and intentions to their social and academic worlds may be more than they are yet capable of doing."[2]

Case goes on to more clearly identify those children who are better candidates for residential care than for traditional approaches by saying, "What separates the most immature teens from their more mature counterparts is that those who are more mature *can shift their entitlement and self-absorption when absolutely necessary. They can . . . accept and respect the needs of others.* Likewise, teens who have poor judgment or who lack realistic expectations are not well-equipped to engage in typical teen exploration."[3]

For most families, Case's thoughts prompt the critical questions: How serious and disruptive are my child's problems to his or her safety, health, and future plans? Have we exhausted all the viable treatment options in our local community? How long have these problems been going on, and are the issues becoming worse? The answers to these questions and observations from an impartial counselor or educator will give you much better insight in your decision about enrolling your child in a residential program.

Finally, of all the problems that adolescents endure in the early part of the twenty-first century, which ones are the most essential to consider when parents are moving toward a decision about sending a child away? Two sociologists from Columbia University, Frederic Reamer and Deborah Siegel, have done an exceptional review of the current research on that question which points to the following factors:

- Excessive and prolonged isolation and withdrawal of the child or adolescent coupled with the feeling that there is no safe adult in his or her life
- Predatory adults in the child's immediate social or educational environment
- School failure and/or truancy, which typically begins in middle school or high school
- Repeated defiance of authority and/or problems in the legal system
- Repeated violent behavior
- Running away
- Negative peer groups
- Highly impulsive behavior, often coupled with self-injury, suicidal ideations, or actual suicide attempts
- Long-term depression
- Drug and/or alcohol abuse
- Eating disorders[4]

Almost every individual making the tough passage from adolescence to adulthood will face one of the factors listed above, but when the factors begin to stack up and no improvement or resolution is in sight, a residential program starts to make sense. Why is it that residential programs often work to help teenagers when community-based approaches don't? Ashley Wade, a former counselor at Acadia Village (now called Village Behavioral Health), a residential treatment facility near Knoxville, Tennessee, put it this way: "When you're working with kids who have significant problems that haven't responded to more traditional approaches, you realize that you need an entire team of people working with the student toward a common therapeutic goal. The teachers, the counselors, the administrators . . . everyone needs to be working in tandem constantly to help the child. It's nearly impossible to get this type of coordinated, cooperative effort on a long-term basis unless your child is in some sort of residential facility."[5] It's the concentration of energy and resources over a long period of time that makes the programs effective. It's an intense and difficult process for the child, the family, and the school's staff as well. This is not summer camp. The good news is that these therapeutic programs, if properly chosen and executed, seem to work.

In the 2006 study by Ellen Behrens and Kristin Satterfield, a thousand students who had been enrolled in residential treatment facilities were surveyed along with their families.[6] The families reported a significant improvement in family relationships, communication, and compliance with parental boundaries after time spent in one of these facilities. There was also a significant reduction of the problems that had led to the children's admission to the schools and programs in the first place. In addition, the children showed marked improvement on each measure of psychosocial functioning and in nearly every clinical syndrome. Keith Russell's long-term research from the University of Minnesota found similar promising results when adolescents and their parents were interviewed three months, six months, and two years after the children's discharge from therapeutic programs.[7*]

In the following chapters, we'll be exploring how to find the right

---

* Readers are cautioned to be aware that research done with surveys can sometimes be skewed toward a more positive outcome than might be seen with other research methods since the people who respond to surveys such as this one typically have had better than average results.

school for your child, how to set realistic expectations about how long the programs will take and how much they'll cost, and how you can sustain your marriage and the rest of your family relationships while your child goes through treatment. Understand that for these therapeutic programs to be effective, your whole family will undergo a transformation—not just your teenager.

chapter 2

Who They Are, Where They Are, and What They Do: A Description of the Different Levels of Therapeutic School Programs

Her name kept coming up everywhere—the educational consul-tant who helped us make Andy's therapeutic school placement. The headmaster at Andy's school gave us her name, Andy's psychiatrist recommended her, and a good friend of ours had worked with her in finding a school for his own son. Our initial meeting with her took place in a conference room that looked like it was designed for a first-tier law firm. She already had reams of school reports and testing data on Andy. She gave us several catalogues with informa-tion about the different therapeutic schools. I knew she was going to help us narrow down our choices about the most appropriate placement for Andy, but I still felt I was drowning in information. The school catalogues were as thick as the ones I'd seen for colleges. How in the world were we going to sort through all the options and get Andy to a school—and quickly? She reassured us. After meet-ing with Andy, reading all his test results, and speaking to Andy's physician and teachers, she already had the field narrowed to seven schools. We took the catalogues home and read them. Our educa-

tion about the therapeutic boarding school industry had begun.
—R. H.

ONCE YOUR FAMILY decides that a therapeutic school is the best treatment option for your child, obviously the next step is to identify which program is going to be the most effective. How in the world do you find the schools that meet your needs in the first place and begin to narrow your choices? An educational consultant can help focus your search quickly. You'll also want to explore the National Association of Therapeutic Schools and Programs (NATSAP) website and its list of affiliated schools at http://natsap.org. To qualify as a NATSAP school, the program must be "licensed by the appropriate state agency authorized to set and oversee standards of therapeutic and/or behavioral healthcare for youth and adolescents or accredited by a nationally recognized behavioral health accreditation agency and to have therapeutic services with oversight by a qualified clinician."[8]

Choosing a NATSAP-affiliated school for your child doesn't give you a 100 percent guarantee that the program will be safe and effective, but it does ensure that the facility is following a clinically sound therapeutic model of "best practices" (we'll discuss the details of "best practices" in chapter 10), and that there is at least some degree of oversight by state regulatory agencies. Remember, though, NATSAP is an industry standard and affiliation, but it is not a formal accreditation. The entire listing of NATSAP affiliates is available free of charge online or by mail.

Several other certification groups exist, such as the Joint Commission (formerly the Joint Commission on Accreditation of Healthcare Organizations, or JCAHO) and the Commission on Accreditation of Rehabilitation Facilities (CARF), which accredit health organizations and behavioral treatment centers to help ensure safe and effective care to consumers. Additionally, organizations such as the Outdoor Behavioral Healthcare Industry Council (OBHIC) and the National Association of Therapeutic Wilderness Camping (NATWC) promote a standard of excellence for wilderness programs and other outdoor behavioral health care facilities. The acronyms and number of agencies can seem overwhelming. The most important thing to remember is that NATSAP is considered the industry standard for therapeutic boarding schools and residential treatment centers. Many NATSAP-affiliated schools and programs also hold an accreditation with the Joint Commission, CARF, or the OBHIC, and others, which add another level of accountability to their programming.

Parents are strongly urged to use caution if they choose to enroll their child in a program or association of schools which "self-certifies" and does not follow therapeutic approaches backed up by solid independent research. Certainly, excellent therapeutic schools are in operation which don't carry the NATSAP seal of approval, and many NATSAP schools would be an inappropriate choice for your child's particular needs, but NATSAP affiliation can at least allay some of your family's anxiety about the care of your child. If you or your educational consultant find a school not affiliated with NATSAP which seems to be a good fit for your child's needs, you'll want to ask why they are not a part of NATSAP or check to see if the facility is in the process of affiliation.

As you do your research about the different schools and programs that are available, you'll run into a whole new vocabulary: *emotional-growth schools, therapeutic boarding schools, residential treatment facilities, wilderness programs, outdoor experiential programs* . . . the verbiage can be confusing at first, and there is often overlap in the definitions and how the schools operate. The schools span a wide continuum not only in the types of problems they address, but also in the intensity of the therapeutic work they do. Below, you'll find a brief description of the different types of programs to give you a better understanding of how each one functions.

WILDERNESS PROGRAMS

Students who are medically stable but present "acting out" behaviors often begin their therapeutic journey in a wilderness program. With most students, "wilderness" is intended to be a short-term intervention, a first step in the recovery process that is generally followed by a referral to an emotional-growth or therapeutic boarding school. Behaviors such as opposition and defiance, substance abuse and dependence, computer and gaming addictions, truancy, and minor legal offenses are typical for students referred to wilderness programs. Therapeutic goals are realized by integrating intensive individual and group therapy in an outdoor setting far removed from the negative distractions of popular culture. In the next chapter, we'll delve into a more in-depth discussion of wilderness therapy.

EMOTIONAL-GROWTH SCHOOLS

Like other therapeutic residential programs, emotional-growth boarding schools are characterized by a structured and supportive therapeutic curriculum. Yet compared to the more intensive psychological curriculum of residential treatment centers (RTCs) and some of the more clinically based therapeutic boarding schools, students in an emotional-growth school generally live in an environment that is less restrictive. The emphasis is on personal responsibility and accountability, which are enhanced by giving students progressively more autonomy to make informed choices. While most emotional-growth schools have therapists who work with the students individually, much of the work is done within the peer group or *milieu*. Guided by experienced program staff and counselors, the students learn about accountability (to themselves and to others), healthy boundaries, and working collaboratively to solve problems within the community. Furthermore, most emotional-growth schools incorporate a family therapy component. Most clinicians agree that a child's therapeutic difficulties are generally a family systems issue and need to be addressed on a family level. Parents can expect their child will be enrolled in an emotional-growth school from twelve to eighteen months, depending on the individual circumstances.

THERAPEUTIC BOARDING SCHOOLS

Considered to be midlevel in the range of therapeutic programming, therapeutic boarding schools (TBSs) move a step beyond emotional-growth schools with increased structure, behavioral support, and clinical sophistication. Generally, a TBS will fall into one of three broad roles for the students referred there.

1. As an initial intervention for students who are not functioning successfully in the home or school environment.
2. As a follow-up step for students who have completed a short-term interventional program such as wilderness therapy.
3. As a step down from a more intensive residential treatment facility.

Individual, group, and family counseling services will typically take up a considerable amount of time during the school week. In addition to general group therapy within the milieu, therapeutic boarding schools offer specialty groups focusing on particular therapeutic issues with topics such as addiction, adoption, grief and loss, and anger management. Therapeutic schools range in size from a dozen students to 120 or more. In addition to programs for adolescents aged thirteen to seventeen, there are also schools specifically for younger children, high school seniors, and young adults. There are single gender and co-ed programs, as well as programs that focus on a specific issue such as drug and alcohol abuse—just to name a few. Many factors have to be considered before a student is enrolled in any program, with the clinical needs of that student being the most critical. As with emotional-growth schools, the length of stay at a TBS is usually a year to eighteen months.

OUTDOOR THERAPEUTIC PROGRAMS
(AS OPPOSED TO WILDERNESS PROGRAMS)

Outdoor therapeutic programs usually fall under the category of thera-peutic boarding schools. These programs are just as clinically and aca-demically sophisticated as other boarding schools that provide dorms or family houses for living arrangements. Students live in rustic cabins or semipermanent yurts in very simple and sparse outdoor environ-ments. Electricity may or may not be available. In winter, the cab-ins are often heated by a wood stove; in summer, they are cooled by Mother Nature or a ceiling fan. Typically, two meals a day are prepared at the campsite (breakfast and dinner) at surprisingly well-maintained and stocked outdoor kitchens. Toilet facilities are often an outhouse-type structure with composting toilets much like the ones you would find at national park campsites. Showers are equally as basic and util-itarian. Students attend school in modern classrooms and eat their midday meal at a traditional school cafeteria. The emphasis is on living a simpler, cleaner life with a minimum of distractions, and students are usually enrolled for twelve to eighteen months.

RESIDENTIAL TREATMENT CENTERS

Increasing in oversight and intensity of therapeutic services provided for students are residential treatment centers (RTCs). Admission to an RTC is reserved for those students who need to be in a clinically inten-sive, closely supervised, and highly structured environment. Residential treatment centers range from interventional hospital-based locked facili-ties to small, nurturing programs with a level of family-like intimacy that belies the clinical intensity of the therapeutic programming. The clinical staff at RTCs are highly trained and often hold advanced psy-chological or medical degrees. All RTCs provide an intense therapeutic curriculum specifically designed to treat the presenting disorders of the students. RTCs include highly specialized programs for eating disorders, substance abuse and other addictions, sexual behavioral issues, sexual trauma, and severe attachment disorder, as well as programs for students with anxiety, depression, and other mood or personality disorders.

RTCs are designed primarily to be interventional, and consequently the typical length of a stay is usually shorter than that for an emotional-growth school or a TBS. In dire life-or-death circumstances, such as with a drug overdose or a suicide attempt, admission to a hospital-based psychiatric facility is warranted, with a length of stay long enough to secure medical stability. Drug rehabilitation typically requires thirty to forty-five days. Families can expect their child's transfer to a longer-term program after the initial rehab where intensive treatment can continue, usually for a period of seven to twelve months. Many students require a step-down program (such as an emotional-growth school or therapeutic boarding school) before the transition back home.

THERAPEUTIC ASSESSMENT PROGRAMS

In some unique and complex situations, a diagnosis or explanation of anomalous behavior in adolescents will not be evident even after significant outpatient or inpatient therapy. In order to make recommendations for long-term placement, admission to a therapeutic assessment program may be the best course of action. These programs are staffed by clinical psychologists, psychiatrists, and therapists who focus on in-depth psychiatric, neuropsychological, and psychoeducational evaluations to gain a comprehensive understanding of the presenting issues. Typically, families can expect their children to stay for testing and observation in these facilities for four to twelve weeks. Once the clinicians and families have clearer insight as to what the core issues are with a student, then recommendations can be made as to which schools are going to be most effective.

PROGRAMS FOR STUDENTS WITH DEVELOPMENTAL DISABILITIES, DELAYS, OR NEUROLOGICAL IMPAIRMENTS

Highly specialized programs, schools, and treatment centers for students with complex diagnoses (or the lack thereof) are also accessible for students and their families. Treatment programs operate for children with impaired neurological functions and/or low cognitive functioning which may be combined with behavioral manifestations such as a trauma or severe anxiety. This category can include programs for students with pervasive developmental disorders (PDDs) such as autism spectrum disorder (ASD), Asperger's syndrome, or nonverbal learning disorder (NLD).

YOUNG ADULT PROGRAMS (FOR STUDENTS OVER EIGHTEEN)

For those students facing the difficult transition to adulthood, young adult programs are most beneficial to ensure success on the path to independent living. Many students are not able to handle the stresses and rigors of college life and fall into patterns of substance abuse, chemical dependency, academic failure, depression, anxiety, and other self-destructive behaviors or mental health disorders. Young adult transition programs provide support—social and emotional, behavioral, and academic—to build confidence and a strong foundation necessary to the health and well-being of their adult students.

For additional information, the NATSAP website provides full descriptions of other specialty therapeutic programs, along with a detailed outline of the principles of good practice to which the organization expects their member schools to adhere.[9]

ACADEMIC CONSIDERATIONS

Not only do these different schools span a wide continuum in the intensity of therapeutic work provided for the students, but they also differ in the types of problems they address. From substance abuse issues to learning disabilities to eating disorders, and for significant mental health issues of nearly every description, there are programs to address these needs—with therapeutic models which recognize that issues with struggling teens seldom stand alone but need to be addressed in sets or clusters of characteristics. There is also a broad range in terms of the academic challenges and expectations for students. A common statement from most of the educators with whom we've spoken in these environments is that it is incredibly difficult for students to function successfully in the classroom if they are emotionally distraught or if their psychological and social needs aren't being adequately addressed. "First things first" is the message we hear over and over again, and the safety and emotional well-being of the child trumps everything else. That being said, however, many emotional-growth and therapeutic boarding schools provide a balance between the clinical program and the academic curriculum. Academic curricula in therapeutic programs range from college preparatory programs to individualized instruction for learning differences to independent study.

One of the parents we interviewed said that her son's academic experience at his therapeutic school had been the strongest component of the program. She said that the structure and rigor of the school's classrooms, coupled with the professionalism of the teachers and low student-to-teacher ratios, gave her son such a boost in confidence academically that it actually made his emotional therapeutic work easier as he transitioned home.

Your child's academic and creative strengths and weaknesses are important factors to weigh as you select a school. Rebecca's step-daughter, Sarah, has the uncanny ability to function at a high level academically even when emotionally she seems brittle, and this ability to "keep ticking" intellectually is one of her greatest strengths—a skill that served her well as she transitioned back to a regular day-school environment. She needed to stay challenged, but not overwhelmed, in the classroom while she was doing her counseling work as well. (In chapter 9 we'll look more closely at the structure of academics within the therapeutic boarding school environments.)

At the emotional-growth-school level of care, group, individual, and family counseling are usually provided in tandem with the overall therapeutic approach of the program, but the frequency of the sessions and the intensity of the work will vary greatly depending on the child's needs and the philosophy of the school. In therapeutic boarding schools and residential treatment centers, as mentioned before, the picture changes. In therapeutic schools, and to an even greater degree in residential treatment centers, individual, group, and family counseling are indicated almost without exception, and those services begin to take up a considerable amount of time during the school week. Additionally, the students' environments become progressively more structured and controlled. Residential treatment centers typically look like emotional-growth or therapeutic schools on the surface, but remember that most RTCs are following a medical model even though they may not look or function like a psychiatric hospital per se.

No matter what level of treatment is appropriate for your family's needs, your child's day-to-day exposure to mass media and popular culture is going to be drastically curtailed. In chapter 7 we'll discuss those changes in greater detail, but you can safely assume that your son or daughter will no longer have open access to e-mail or Facebook, to MP3 players, cell phones, video games, or even television or radio—at least not at first. Access to those types of electronic entertainment is often considered a privilege that has to be earned by the student, and there are facilities where even seeing a daily newspaper or watching movies is significantly restricted until the final stages of the treatment program.

Educators and clinicians in the therapeutic school arena have a strong rationale for limiting this exposure, and we'll explore those reasons more fully in chapter 6, but losing social networking and the wireless world is a jolt for most of the students, and it takes a bit of getting used to for the rest of the family as well. The days of being able to pick up your cell phone and chat with your son or daughter, send a text, or to communicate through Skype or Facebook (assuming he or she would ever confirm you as a friend in the first place) are gone for a while. It can be an isolating adjustment on both sides.

Likewise, the dress codes at most therapeutic schools and RTCs are fairly strict, although few require a school uniform. Students and parents will be provided with clear and straightforward information from the schools before enrollment about what clothing is considered appropriate and what the rules are on cosmetics, jewelry, haircuts, and body piercings. As you might imagine, the guidelines are typically much more conservative and restrictive than the expectations were at home or in a regular day-school environment. In residential treatment centers, even access to everyday grooming tools such as razors or curling irons may be restricted, since these implements could be used for self-harm or to injure other people.

Now that you're armed with the formal definitions of what the schools provide at different levels of therapeutic care, the most important question becomes which level of care and which therapeutic approach is going to be the most appropriate and effective for your child. At this point, it's time to call in the pros (assuming you haven't done so already). Selecting the appropriate school for your child without thorough assessment by a psychologist or psychiatrist and without the guidance of an experienced educational consultant is a bit like preparing a complicated tax return without the help of an accountant. You can do it, but your chances of making a serious mistake with long-term negative consequences are high. Remember, however, that no affiliation with a professional organization or oversight by a government agency is a substitute for your own research and scrutiny in choosing a school. Consultants, physicians, and counselors can guide you in your choice, but the ultimate decision and responsibility for the choice belongs to the parents.

Ideally, parents should tour the schools and facilities they are considering for their child. *Ideally,* parents would be able to meet with key administrators, teachers, and lead therapists before the final decision on placement is made. And *ideally,* parents should have a chance to talk with several students at the school without staff supervision to get their input on the strengths and weaknesses of the program. The ideal, unfortunately, is not always possible. You know already how difficult, expensive, and time-consuming researching and visiting schools can be, especially when your child is experiencing the type of turmoil at home that makes the consideration of therapeutic schools an option in the first place. Educational consultants become an invaluable resource in your search at this point. They tour the schools they recommend—as well as the ones they don't—on a regular basis, and they'll be able to help you narrow your search significantly and give you firsthand reports about conditions and staff at the schools if you aren't able to visit yourself.

In the next chapter we'll investigate how outdoor therapeutic or wilderness programs fit into the overall plan for your child's treatment.

chapter 3

Beyond This There Be Dragons: Dispelling the Myths about Wilderness Education

Top 10 Things I Learned from Wilderness Education

10. Best to keep your bug spray at the top of the pack, not at the very bottom! Bugs go for the sweetest smelling thing around. But after a couple of days, they'll leave you alone. Frustration!

9. Your fingernails will get filthy after only a couple of hours, but you become the cleanest you've ever been—physically and emotionally. Resilience!

8. It's hard work, and learning to "bust a coal" for fire is even harder. Perseverance!

7. You laugh and have fun, and "busting a coal" makes you smile even more! Success! (Then perhaps you celebrate with banana pudding made from banana chips? Creativity!)

6. You don't really hang bears when you do the "bear hang." (All programs swear they have heard this—a true wilder-

ness legend.) This is what you do to keep the critters out of your food. Teamwork!

5. You cry, you're angry, you're afraid, you shut down, but comfort can be just around the next bend. Friendship!

4. The wilderness staff care deeply about you. They nurture you when you're sad, hold boundaries when you're over the line. They ask you hard questions. Expectations!

3. You're safe.

2. Your children enter hurt and unhappy, but leave strong and healing and happy. Empowerment!

1. Your children learn to be children again. They love you and they need you. Trust!

—E. D.

JUST AS PEOPLE in the Middle Ages were terrified of sailing off the edge of the earth or scared of finding dragons beyond the boundaries of their maps, parents of struggling teenagers today are equally anxious and worried about all the unknown and unpredictable situations they'll encounter as they begin the therapeutic process with their child. Today's dragons are real and much more frightening than any mythical beast of the past.

For many adolescents, the introduction to the therapeutic boarding school process begins with a phase called wilderness. Wilderness is a proverbial bucket of water poured over the head, a shake of the shoulders, a loud and clear wake-up call to a child that his or her actions and choices are destructive and unacceptable. It's a message from the parents and the other concerned adults in an adolescent's life that negative behaviors must and will change.

The decision to intervene in such a profound manner doesn't come easily. Educational and mental health professionals fully understand the benefits of wilderness therapy intervention, but parents are often and understandably apprehensive about the whole process. The Internet is rife with horror stories about "boot camps" that subject students to extreme, harsh, and often punitive environments. Some of those programs still exist, and it's the referring professionals' mandate to provide detailed information to the parents in order to avoid these unethical and potentially dangerous placements. The types of wilderness programs we'll discuss in this chapter do *not* fall under the "boot camp" category. In the simplest terms, wilderness is an extended backcountry camping trip, but of course, it's much more than that. Here's how it works: Typically without forewarning, the child is escorted either by his parents or by a professional transport team with little more than the clothes on his back and promptly delivered to a base camp, where he receives an orientation from trained counselors about why he is there and what he is in for. If, upon arrival at base camp and after a thorough medical evaluation, there is evidence of significant drug and alcohol addiction with potentially serious withdrawal effects, the staff may consider medical detoxification at another facility. Most hospitals can safely and securely implement an intensive, short-term treatment plan for drug and alcohol withdrawal. It is imperative that the student be as healthy as possible before joining the group in the field.

Quickly, the child is "on the trail," learning how to pitch a tent, make a campfire (or "bust a coal," as it's often called on the trail), and cook and take care of his or her own health and hygiene under the most basic conditions. The wilderness program will provide everything the student needs on the trail in terms of camping equipment, clothing, and food.

The students learn teamwork, cooperation, accountability, and personal responsibility along with the practical skills of how to sustain themselves physically in the outdoors for an extended period of time. The concepts and practices of group therapy may be introduced formally, or they may flow from the natural schedule and demands of a backpacking experience. It's a profound experience for most teenagers. They are dealing with a new parent now—Mother Nature, the toughest but most impartial authority figure of all. She doesn't pick favorites, but she doesn't take excuses or rationalization from anyone either. It's impossible to negotiate with her. The adolescents hike, they climb, they boulder (which is climbers' slang for a scrambling hike over large rocks and obstacles), they raft and canoe, they even ski and snowshoe in certain areas, all the while participating in a therapeutic environment where each person is responsible for his or her own behavior and where he or she can clearly and quickly see how individual actions affect the entire group.

To reiterate, this is a time and place of serious work, not simply a camping excursion. The primary goals of wilderness are simple and straightforward:

- To show the students the natural consequences of their behavior while they are outside their comfort zone
- To build self-confidence by way of mastery of outdoor survival skills

For many students, the supportive peer group of wilderness and the success they experience in mastering practical skills on the trail go a long way in building the strength and self-esteem they'll need in the rest of the therapeutic process. The child learns quickly that while she can't prevent the rain, she can pitch a tent to get out of the rain. She's going to need the help of her teammates to get the tent up quickly, and no one can do her part for her. The team needs her; she is critical to the effort.

Even though the students come from all over the country and from a wide range of socioeconomic backgrounds, most of their underlying issues are the same. In the wilderness experience, the cultural reality is radically changed, offering the adolescent the opportunity to consider his or her actions and attitudes in a whole new light. Typically wilderness programs are four to twelve weeks in length, and while some students will be ready to return home to regular day-school environments and traditional therapeutic regimens afterward, most of the adolescents will need to enroll in emotional-growth or therapeutic boarding schools post-wilderness to practice and reinforce the new skills and thinking patterns they've learned on the trail. Most educators and counselors agree that children should *go straight into their therapeutic boarding school placement* instead of going home first.[10]

In only a few weeks, most students have made substantial progress toward overcoming significant emotional (and physical) obstacles. They have a newfound sense of peace and self-confidence. They are clean, sober, on an emotional high. Even a short trip home can stir up old resentments and hurts—a visit risks a setback on the path to recovery and healing. While it is incredibly important for the adolescent to reconnect with his or her family, this reunification needs to happen in a safe, neutral environment. This is not a time for a fancy vacation to reward a "job well done." In many situations, a day or two at a mountain cabin or moderately priced hotel to clean up, share experiences, and reconnect with parents and siblings can make the transition to the next placement a more seamless experience. Of course, there are those students who are best served by an immediate transition to the next therapeutic school or program. Circumstances are highly individualized, and consultation is needed before a post-wilderness plan is implemented.

Several of Andy's classmates in Montana said that while they were upset and frustrated that they couldn't go home directly after completing their wilderness programs, they were so delighted to have hot meals, hot showers, and a regular bed to sleep in after weeks of camping that they didn't complain for too long about their follow-up treatment (the post-wilderness placements are often referred to as "after-care"). After only a few weeks in wilderness, the students' shifts in priorities had already taken root.

Wilderness leaders are a hearty bunch. Most field staff, especially the team leaders, have strong academic backgrounds and clinical training in psychology. They are also certified in first aid and first responder techniques. They have to know what they're doing not only in fastening a belay harness for rock climbing or showing the students how to purify stream water, but also in leading, motivating, and controlling a small band of campers who almost certainly don't want to be there. They are completely entrusted with the children's health and safety during the wilderness experience when the students will have little, if any, direct contact with their families.

Most wilderness programs for adolescents are single-gender, while coeducational groups are more common for young adults and younger adolescents. The number of students in a group can range from three to more than a dozen, but experienced wilderness directors consistently recommend a 3:1 student-to-staff ratio on the trail.[11] With all the challenges of the wilderness experience, this appropriate ratio and staff training are critical.

When wilderness therapy programs first came into use, parents and clinicians had limited options in terms of what clinical components were utilized in this initial part of treatment. Today, however, families have access to several models of wilderness therapy to select from. Your educational consultant or other referring professional will guide you through the process of selecting the best model for your child, giving you information about the efficacy of difference approaches for specific issues. Whether located in the desert, on a mountaintop, or in the tropics, the programs share a common philosophy: to intervene—safely—and to break the cycle of destructive behavior that is consuming the child's life and well-being. Wilderness is about learning to live in community; it's about learning accountability to oneself and to others.

With the emergence of so many niche programs, it has become even more important to understand the nuances underpinning the individual program philosophies. Qualified educational consultants once again are indispensable to families at this juncture. They make it their business to understand those program nuances and to make placement recommendations based on the specific circumstances of the student and family.

In the past, wilderness therapy often meant bare-bones, hardscrabble trekking in the mountains or the deserts of the American West. Many excellent programs continue to follow this original format with great success, and they remain a viable option for many youth. However, building on the foundation of the early program philosophies, wilderness therapy has evolved into a more comprehensive treatment model drawing from the time-tested basis of simple and healthy living. From remote forests in Maine to the tropical lushness of Hawaii, and everywhere in between, wilderness programs now include curricular components such as adventure trekking, sustainable farming, yoga, meditation and mindfulness training, nutrition and wellness, and other treatment modalities. Furthermore, programs exist for students with significant learning disabilities, including Asperger's syndrome and other autism spectrum disorders. Several programs have access to licensed medical personnel in the field and can manage conditions such as diabetes or asthma. The clinical expertise that has evolved is remarkable, but wilderness still maintains its effectiveness in its simple, theoretical model of safe intervention.

TYPES OF WILDERNESS THERAPY PROGRAMS

Base Camp versus Nomadic Models

Base camp facilities are usually constructed as a primitive camp environment in remote locations with basic shower and toilet structures. Rustic cabins, yurts, or teepees are available in the case of severe weather, but typically students make camp much as they do while on expedition. In some states, such as North Carolina, wilderness programs are required by law to operate as a base camp model. In a normal cycle, students spend two to three days in base camp and then four to seven days on expedition. While at base, the emphasis is on basic needs such as personal hygiene, doing laundry, catching up on academic and therapeutic assignments, and having the students meet individually with their therapists.

Although being at base can bring respite from the arduous days spent hiking and working through daily life on the trail, this model is not Wilderness Lite. Real work is done here just as it is in the backcountry. The focus remains on learning to live, work, and play in *community*—just as many therapeutic moments can be had here as in the field. As the cycle progresses, anticipation builds, nerves are often on edge, and tempers flare as the students prepare, once again, to make the long trek back into the wilderness.

In a nomadic model, after an initial medical check and/or observation and orientation phase, students are transported to their groups in the field. Group dynamics are ever-changing as new, incoming students replace students who have progressed to graduation. In a nomadic model, students remain in the field, generally cut off from the influences of the outside world, for the duration of their stay.

Weekly staff changes and overnight visits from parents or referring professionals bring excitement to the camp—the kids are always eager for news and information. However, these visits can present challenges to the group, and they are carefully planned, as some students are particularly adept at manipulating and dramatizing events of the past week in an effort to garner sympathy and perhaps (in their minds) to finagle a quick ticket home. Nope. The students may be wily, but the field staff have seen and heard it all before.

Some programs lease or own land where they have set up several semipermanent, rudimentary campsites. Several groups will be in fairly close proximity to each other, but never close enough for the groups to comingle. Again, basic shower and toilet facilities may be located nearby, but nothing can be accessed easily or without group planning. Other programs gain permits from the Bureau of Land Management to access federal and state-owned parklands for camping and trekking. Federal regulations require that the programs "leave no trace."

Although the field staff have favorite areas to set up as campsites, nothing is permanent, and literally everything that is brought has to be removed before the team can move on to the next site.

Adventure Therapy

Most wilderness therapy programs base their therapeutic curriculum on a backcountry expedition model. Recently, however, several programs have moved beyond the traditional model to include other outdoor experiential activities such as kayaking, caving, and rock climbing, among others. The emphasis remains firmly planted in implementing safe intervention, learning responsibility and accountability, and learning how to live in community, but now those things can be learned with snowshoes strapped on! Therapy happens whether it's on the trail or on a mountain bike, whether with hiking boots or with cross-country skis. With all wilderness therapy models, the underlying therapeutic philosophy is learning to trust and make good decisions in an environment that is not coercive or punitive. With the adventure therapy model, the hope is that students will learn to build confidence and self-efficacy in ways that will be effective once they leave the program. It's common knowledge that engaging in physical activity can increase endorphins, which are chemicals that trigger the pleasure receptors in the brain. Physical activity is beneficial not only for physical fitness, but also for mental fitness.

The success of the high-adventure component of these programs, the "thrill seeking," if you will, gives credence to some of the most current research in neuroscience, which proposes that the risk-taking and impulsive, dangerous decisions so many adolescents make are actually a natural part of their cognitive development that propels them to independence and adulthood.[12] The key is to keep the adolescents safe, alive, and healthy while their frontal lobes finish cooking! Adventure therapy allows the thrill seeking to take place in supervised, relatively safe activities such as whitewater rafting or rock climbing instead of with drugs, alcohol, violence, or promiscuity.

Multidimensional Programs

If needed, your educational consultant can help you identify and locate specialty, niche programs that will meet your child's specific problems. For instance, *equine therapy components* are especially effective for children who have been adopted, who have attachment-related disorders, or who have deficits in verbal communication. Equine-assisted therapy is an accepted and successful treatment modality. Horses are extremely social animals who communicate their feelings to each other through body language. Humans communicate subtly in much the same way. Horses have an uncanny ability to mirror what human body language is telling them. Learning to read a horse's body language correlates strongly to the ability to read human interaction. In equine therapy, students learn to establish trust, build self-confidence, and develop effective communication skills that are necessary to building successful relationships with other people. (We'll focus more on adoption issues and attachment disorders in chapter 14.)

Programs for low cognitive or autism spectrum disorder students: Group dynamics in any wilderness program are challenging as students learn to live in community, but with the inherent social deficits of students on the autism spectrum or students with significant cognitive disabilities, life skills instruction—not to mention therapeutic work—becomes a special challenge for clinicians and students alike. Not only do these struggling youth have to figure out the group dynamics, but they have to find a way to celebrate their individuality and talents, often after living in environments where they were bullied and denigrated. Fortunately, several wilderness programs have realized the special needs of this group of students and have created safe havens for a positive peer experience and personal growth while staying true to the overarching wilderness therapy goal of safe intervention.

In *combination wilderness and academic semester programs,* the students live in dorms and take academic classes for most of the week but go on regular camping expeditions for three or four days at a time and also engage in group and individual counseling sessions. *Solo treks* are also available for students. In this type of backcountry adventure trekking the entire program is individualized to meet the specific needs of the family. Programs also exist with a strong focus on farming, yoga, meditation, and other wellness practices.

A wilderness experience won't be necessary or recommended for every student beginning the journey through the therapeutic boarding school process, and completion of a wilderness trek doesn't mean that the student won't go back for more time on the trail. It's uncommon, but some emotional-growth or therapeutic schools will recommend that an adolescent go back for a wilderness *refresher* if he or she becomes overly unruly, defiant, or can't abide by the rules of the school program.

For a small number of students, wilderness is clearly not appropriate. If the child does not have adequate cognitive skills or physical strength, if the student is medically fragile or is noncompliant in dealing with an illness such as diabetes, or if he or she is exhibiting suicidal tendencies, wilderness may not be a good option. If a child is under acute stress or is dealing with complex psychiatric issues, he or she will need to be screened closely before a placement decision in wilderness is made. For those students, a short-term hospitalization to establish greater stability or a referral to a program that focuses on evaluation and assessment in a residential setting may be a better way to begin the therapeutic process.

For the majority of students for whom wilderness is recommended, however, the time and experience on the trail not only gives the child a chance to build confidence and a cooperative approach to tasks, it also gives the wilderness leaders and the clinical staff an opportunity for more thorough observation of the child's problems and strengths. Some of the larger mental health organizations, such as CRC Health Group and Aspen Education Group, have their own wilderness programs which may feed directly into one of their schools or residential treatment centers after the child has finished with the experiential, outdoor portion of his or her work, but program directors and educational consultants will work with families on a one-on-one basis to select the appropriate follow-up facilities.

MOVING YOUR CHILD INTO A WILDERNESS PROGRAM

Your child is in trouble . . . perhaps legally, emotionally, or educationally, with drugs or alcohol, or most likely with an exhausting combination of these issues. Chances are he or she is not in a position of great clarity to recognize the need for wilderness and/or a follow-up therapeutic setting. How does a parent get a child out of a toxic situation and into a wilderness program? These teenagers are not preschoolers that parents can pick up and put in time-out for five minutes. Often, our children are bigger and stronger, at least physically, than we are. Some of our children, such as Andy, can be convinced to enter treatment or go to wilderness of their own volition, but often parents need help escorting their children to these programs, and that help is available. It's called *transport,* and your educational consultant or the program administrators at the schools you are considering will help your family arrange for these services.

Some Internet bloggers have called the transport companies nothing more than "paid kidnappers," but the consensus among most parents, educational consultants, and therapeutic program directors is that appropriately vetted and licensed transport services have tremendous integrity and that staff members treat the students they are moving with dignity and respect. Parents have to be mindful, obviously, that the vast majority of young people being transported to therapeutic programs will be in shock about the process and won't want to go. The individuals who work in the transport process have to be meticulously trained and experienced in working with adolescents and crisis intervention. Transport personnel come from all walks of life, but not surprisingly, many have previously worked in law enforcement or in therapeutic educational environments. Regulation and licensing requirements vary from region to region, but in states such as California, transport companies are required to be registered with Trust-Line, an independent agency that runs full background checks on all employees. Transport personnel will be trained in CPR, de-escalation techniques, and the appropriate use of physical restraint protocols if your child becomes violent or abusive.

The consensus with most educational consultants and therapists is *not to deceive your child about the circumstances of transport*. It's better not to tell him or her anything at all, especially if you think your child may try to run away to avoid transport, than it is to lie about what is getting ready to happen. Andy and one of his close friends from a residential treatment center had unbelievable, fantastic stories about the ruses parents used to trick their adolescents into transport delivery. One student thought his parents were taking him out for an early morning breakfast, only to find the transport van in the parking lot of the neighborhood McDonald's. One family told their daughter they were crossing over into Canada from the United States to take advantage of the good exchange rates for shopping, when in reality they were taking her to a wilderness program located on the Canadian border. Don't lie; otherwise you'll have an enormous trust deficit to repay with your children as they progress with their therapeutic programs.

Remember, wilderness therapy is all about the *initiation of change*. Some students, after completing their time on the trail, will look back on the experience and say that wilderness was the most positive, life-changing event of their lives. Some won't want to leave. Other adolescents will resent being sent away against their will into such Spartan conditions, and they'll bring that anger with them when they begin after-care in a therapeutic school or an RTC. Either way, the process of change has already started at some level, and the students as well as their parents will realize that real change is within their grasp. That sense of empowerment will be a critical factor for success in the rest of the therapeutic process.

chapter 4

The Genesis of the Therapeutic Boarding School Industry

I was sitting in a parents' workshop for Sarah. The treatment team from her emotional-growth school in North Carolina was presenting two full days of information about the program goals and the therapeutic models they were using with our children. I knew this was a well-established program and protocol; the strategies these counselors were using had been refined over years. But how, I wondered, had these programs gotten started in the first place? I asked the lead therapist during the question-and-answer session, but her response wasn't satisfying to me. I searched on the Internet when I got back from having dinner with Sarah that night, but I couldn't find much. Once I got back to Atlanta, I had a meeting with our educational consultant. She gave me a name, Mel Wasserman, and told me about the CEDU programs. Now I had the keys I needed to do my research.   —*R. H.*

IN 1990, WHEN NATSAP was just getting organized, there were about fifty emotional-growth boarding schools and wilderness education programs in the country. By 2000, the number of schools had grown to more than a hundred, and by the end of 2007, the number of schools had doubled again to more than two hundred NATSAP-affiliated schools.[13] In its explosive growth, the industry was simply responding to market demand.* In a 2006 Centers for Disease Control and Prevention study on youth risk behavior, researchers presented some troubling statistics. In the population of teenagers they surveyed across the country and from a wide variety of socio-economic backgrounds they found that 16.9 percent had seriously considered suicide in the previous twelve months, and in that same time frame:

- 9.9 percent had driven drunk or stoned
- 7.5 percent had been sexually assaulted
- 7.6 percent had used cocaine
- 18.5 percent had carried a weapon[14]

The pressures of going through adolescence and growing up appear to be becoming more dangerous and intense. Clearly there was and is a growing need for emotional-growth and therapeutic schools. But how did the schools get started?

Not surprisingly, the genesis for these types of programs grew out of the social turmoil of the late 1960s. The founder of the first therapeutic schools, however, was the most unlikely pioneer imaginable. His name was Mel Wasserman, and he was a furniture salesman from Palm Springs, California. It was the mid-1960s, and Wasserman would often leave his store for a few minutes to have lunch at the small restaurant just down the street. The restaurant was directly across from the public library, and from his table, Wasserman and the other customers could see the steps of the library where college students gathered to protest the Vietnam War and the other political and social problems facing our country at the time.

---

* The number of therapeutic schools without NATSAP affiliation was also growing, but those numbers are difficult, if not impossible, to track.

Wasserman watched as many of the students became aggressive and confrontational with the drivers and pedestrians who came by. He got curious and concerned. He began engaging the students, talking to them about their causes, their opinions, and eventually their personal lives and struggles. Many of the students had problems with drug abuse and addiction, and many of them were completely estranged from their families. It wasn't long before Wasserman and his wife, Brigitte, were inviting the protesters for meals and conversation in their home. To those who were living on the streets, Wasserman would offer a safe place to stay and meals in exchange for some chores or odd jobs around the Wasserman's store or home. More young people came, and then more . . . and they stayed longer and longer. "Finally," many of them said, "we've found an adult who will listen."[15] Even though Mel Wasserman had no formal training in education or psychology, he found himself the *de facto* director of an alternative education and rehabilitation program.

By 1967, Wasserman had sold his furniture store and established the first of his CEDU schools. The four-letter acronym, pronounced see-doo, doesn't correspond to a specific school name or therapeutic approach. Instead it simply means, "*see* yourself as you are and *do* something about it." Former CEDU students have speculated that the acronym was actually Wasserman's acknowledgment of a man named Charles E. Dietrich and his influence on Wasserman's programs, but there is no evidence of this in any of the sources about the early therapeutic schools.[16]

As his work expanded, Wasserman surrounded himself with educators and therapists who had the professional training and experience he lacked. Unfortunately, he also drew practitioners with questionable credentials and methods into his circle and treatment teams. From the first months of the program until the final days of the CEDU schools nearly forty years later, Wasserman's educational philosophy and methods were always draped in controversy. Even today, decades later, Mel Wasserman and his methods continue to draw ire and criticism from professionals in the therapeutic school community and from his former students.

Wasserman's original therapeutic approach borrowed heavily from an adult rehabilitation program that was started in Santa Monica, California, in 1958 called Synanon. Synanon's founder was the man we mentioned before, Charles Dietrich, who was a reformed alcoholic and respected speaker at Alcoholics Anonymous meetings. Dietrich branched off from AA in an attempt to start a program that responded to the needs of drug addicts as well as alcoholics. Synanon's focus was on group therapy and "truth-telling sessions," which later became known as "The Game" or "The Synanon Game." Participants in the group sessions were required to be brutally honest with themselves and with each other, holding their fellow group members to complete accountability for their actions and feelings. Wasserman employed a milder version of The Game in the group counseling sessions he had for young adults and adolescents, but the basic philosophy remained the same.[17]

Even with the constant criticism of Wasserman's methods, the CEDU focus on adherence to boundaries and personal accountability found a large, accepting audience with parents, educators, and the court systems throughout the '70s and '80s. Wasserman's credo is clearly articulated in a quote he often used with parents and students in orientation settings: "Take away boundaries and you bring in a sewer, a biker society. The magic of our program is not in this building . . . it is in the setting of boundaries—and the posture and the certain way we act within those boundaries and posture . . . it's in that place we have something which facilitates what we are trying to do (for our clients)."[18]

According to an interview with a former CEDU staff member, in the early days of the program there was constant friction between the California Department of Public Health, which wanted to shut down Wasserman's facility since CEDU didn't have the proper school licensing or building codes, and the California court system, which wanted

Wasserman up and operating since the courts saw CEDU as a viable alternative to prison for young, nonviolent offenders.[19]

After a few years, the Wasserman program outgrew its original space in Palm Springs, and the school moved to a larger campus called Running Springs, which was located near San Bernardino, California. The original Palm Springs location and the Running Springs school focused their work on young adults in their early to mid-twenties. However, it became clear to Wasserman and his colleagues as they worked with this age group that earlier intervention was needed for the types of problems they were encountering with their students. In the early 1980s, the first CEDU program was established for high school students.

By 1982, CEDU had opened a second school in eastern Washington state called Rocky Mountain Academy, and in 1987 an affiliate program that would later join the CEDU family of schools, the now-defunct Mount Bachelor Academy, was established in Prineville, Oregon. In less than three years CEDU added a middle school at the original Running Springs campus to address the problems of younger students, and in 1993, yet another CEDU school, Boulder Creek Academy, began operation and treatment programs. Every year the demand for therapeutic boarding schools increased across the country, and CEDU, along with other programs and schools, responded by adding more programs.

As the number of children receiving psychotropic medications (such as those used for treating ADD/ADHD, depression, bipolar disorder, and other problems) increased radically during the late 1980s and 1990s, CEDU adapted its admissions policies and began accepting large numbers of students who were receiving these types of medications. Another significant change and addition to the CEDU programs came in 1994 when Ascent, a therapeutic wilderness program, was opened in conjunction with CEDU's Northwest Academy in Idaho. In the '90s, CEDU began experiencing financial difficulty and a growing number of complaints against the school and staff members for mistreatment of students. In 1996, CEDU filed for bankruptcy protection, and the schools were sold.*

While the CEDU programs were eventually closed, other schools and programs grounded in the concepts that Wasserman introduced continued to thrive, and wilderness education was integrated more and more into the therapeutic boarding school protocol. The rationale for using wilderness education as a part of the therapeutic process grew out of the work of a German-born educator named Kurt Hahn, who founded the Outward Bound movement in the early days of World War II.

If Mel Wasserman's credentials and methods raised eyebrows in professional circles, Kurt Hahn's reputation was on the other side of the spectrum. His background, from an educational perspective, was impeccable. Born in 1886 in Berlin to Jewish parents, Hahn studied at Oxford, at Berlin, and at universities in Heidelberg, Freiburg, and Göttingen. In 1920 he founded Schule Schloss Salem, a private boarding school where he served as headmaster until 1933. Hahn protested vigorously against the rising power and violence of the Nazi Party, and his vocal opposition soon led to his imprisonment. After an appeal by the British prime minister, Hahn was released from prison and allowed to immigrate to Scotland. Once there, Hahn went on to found Gordonstoun, a school closely modeled on the educational principles he used at Schule Schloss Salem.

Hahn believed that children and adolescents possessed an innate moral decency, but that morality was often corrupted by society as the children grew older (ironically, this appeared to be true in 1920 as well as today). Hahn reasoned that if students were exposed to an education that gave them opportunities for personal leadership and

---

* Boulder Creek Academy and Northwest Academy are still in existence today. However, both of these programs operate under a completely different philosophy than the CEDU schools of the past. They are currently owned and operated by Universal Health Services and are highly respected in the realm of residential therapeutic schools and programs.

showed them directly the results of their choices, then their sense of personal integrity could be preserved or restored. At the base of Hahn's philosophy were concern and compassion for others, willingness to accept personal responsibility, and the tenacious pursuit of truth. In Hahn's estimation, punishment of any sort should be used only as a last resort.

Kurt Hahn wrote extensively about the decline of youth after World War I, and he offered four educational solutions to remedy the problems. The first precept was fitness training, which he saw as an avenue to challenge, self-discipline, and increased determination. Next came "expeditions," where students used their physical fitness in long, challenging endurance tasks. For the third area of education, Hahn wanted to see the students intensively involved in improving their manual skills; he believed this training would give them a stronger sense of competence and problem-solving abilities. Finally, Hahn wanted his students to look outward and serve others through first aid, fire fighting, or surf lifesaving.

In 1941, Hahn and British shipping magnate Sir Lawrence Holt took the character education principles of the Gordonstoun School out of the classroom and onto the North Sea. Young sailors in the British Royal Navy preparing to fight in World War II were given the skills training and experience necessary for their survival and the survival of their shipmates using Hahn's teaching methods. The program was named Outward Bound after the nautical expression for ships leaving the safety and certainty of the harbor.[20]

The Outward Bound movement found its way to the United States in the early 1950s when one of Kurt Hahn's protégés and a teacher at the Gordonstoun School, Josh Miner, introduced the concepts formally to American educators. In 1961 the first US-based Outward Bound school was opened, and it spawned a nationwide consortium of experiential education later to be known as wilderness. Of course, Outward Bound is not used exclusively in therapeutic settings. Mainstream schools, universities, camps, and corporations use Outward

Bound or similar programs for team building and the promotion of self-reliance in a wide range of academic and business settings.

The blending of Outward Bound principles to the therapeutic arena came out of the work of Larry Olsen and Ezekiel Sanchez, the founders of the ANASAZI Foundation. The goal of ANASAZI, as posted on their website, is "preparing parents and children to turn their hearts to one another, begin anew, and walk in harmony in the wilderness of the world."[21] Larry Olsen's childhood love of Native American culture and survival camping grew into a career as he began teaching classes in outdoor survival in the continuing education program at Brigham Young University. Through that experience, he was able to field test his methods on thousands of university students, and the results were remarkable. Not only were his students able to live off the land and survive, they also developed courage, self-confidence, and a strong sense of community through team building.

One of Olsen's students was Ezekiel Sanchez, the son of migrant farm workers and the first in his family to finish high school and go on to college. A Totonac Indian, Sanchez possessed a phenomenal tracking ability, survival skills, and understanding of native plants and herbs that earned him a heroic reputation with his classmates and teachers. Olsen recognized the talent. He invited Sanchez to develop courses and curriculum for BYU's program, and Sanchez became a full-time staff member and teacher for BYU's Department of Youth Leadership. Sanchez left the university after church leaders asked him to implement a similar program in the remote areas of the Navajo Indian Reservation. During the summer months, however, Sanchez and Olsen continued working together on youth outdoor programs, and in 1988 they established the ANASAZI Foundation. By applying the Anasazi tribe's principles of living simply in harmony with the land and other people, the foundation became the first program in the nation of its kind to be licensed and nationally accredited as a behavioral health care provider. Sanchez and Olsen are widely recognized as the grandfathers of wilderness education programs in the United States.[22]

Wilderness education programs have become some of the most dynamic and innovative areas in therapeutic treatment with new venues and delivery systems available to families. Educational consultants are exceptionally busy, visiting and vetting these programs to see which ones will be most effective for their clients. The expansion of options is an exciting development in the therapeutic realm, allowing for even more specific and individualized treatment even as the underlying goals remain the same.

chapter 5

Shepherds in the Desert:
The Role of Educational Consultants
and How to Find One

After a frigid night in the remote woods of northern Wisconsin, a snowmobile ride seemed like just the thing to shake off the fog of my sleep-deprived brain. I climbed on and off we went, slowly at first, as my guide made sure that he wasn't going to bounce me off the back. We sped along a forest service trail, nothing but a winter wonderland surrounding us until we reached a frozen lake, one of literally hundreds in this part of the wilderness.

"The boys' camp is just across the lake," my guide said as we set off on foot.

I was a little nervous, as I'm not used to walking on ice, but I did have crampons on my boots. After a few minutes on the hard pack, all seemed well. We clomped along and talked and laughed—I'm sure all part of the guide's plan to distract me from what lay ahead.

Schlump! Suddenly, in one short step, I was up to mid-calf in slushy snow and ice. I looked around and there we were, stuck in the middle of this vast whiteness, in the middle of what was surely a not-quite-frozen lake. Needless to say, I was petrified.

"I guess we should have brought snowshoes," my fearless guide remarked as he grinned from ear to ear. Steady on his feet and with an outstretched hand he asked, "Do you trust me? Take my hand and I'll help you get to the other side."

I thought about my options. I could trust him and move forward to explore new places, or I could do the known thing, backtrack, and be right where I started. As he explained, the slushiness was from the melting and refreezing of snow and ice, and there was still probably sixteen inches of frozen lake under my feet. It took a while and I almost lost a boot once or twice, but we made it to the boys' camp—certainly an adventure I'll never forget.

In retrospect, I realize that what happened to me on that cold day in February draws a direct parallel to what I do in my educational consulting practice. With every client, the implied question is, "Do you trust me? Take my hand and I'll help you get to the other side." For most people, this requires a huge leap of faith to develop that level of trust, often in a very short period of time. That's why I need to do everything that I can to make sure that I have the knowledge and expertise, I have the connections, and I continue to have the empathy necessary to be an effective advocate for my young clients. —E. D.

ONE OF THE most valuable resources a family can have as they try to find an appropriate treatment program and school for their child is the expertise and advice of a trained educational consultant. These professionals, who often have backgrounds in education and/or psychology, can help you determine what level of treatment is needed for the student and which facilities are going to be best suited for your family's needs. A good educational consultant should also be able to help you determine what other testing or observation needs to be done, if possible, before your child enters an emotional-growth school or experiential wilderness program.

Educational consultants visit the full spectrum of schools and residential treatment centers throughout the year for updates and evaluations, and they follow the same practice in reviewing wilderness programs. To qualify for Independent Educational Consultants Association (IECA) membership, individuals must fulfill an exhaustive list of requirements, one of which is to make initial visits to fifty or more therapeutic centers and then to follow up with campus visits to at least twenty-five different programs for "troubled teens" annually. Most educational consultants (or IECs, as they frequently call themselves) far exceed the minimum requirements, often visiting seventy or more programs on a yearly basis. Frequently, Elizabeth spends time in the field with groups of students and counselors, living the wilderness experience right along with them. Researching and writing about the wilderness experience is one thing. Living in a tent with no running water for weeks at a time brings a whole new level of clarity and expertise to describing the endeavor.

How do you go about finding an effective educational consultant? Often psychiatrists, psychologists, or school counselors will be able to provide you with a referral. Or you can search on your own through the Independent Educational Consultants Association website: www. iecaonline.com.

Educational consultants work in a wide variety of settings with a diverse client base. Naturally, you'll want to work with someone who specializes in placing children in therapeutic environments as opposed to a consultant who helps families with college applications, admissions, or routine private school admissions—although many IECs hold specialty designations in several areas. In addition to helping families find the right therapeutic placements, educational consultants can also be invaluable in helping students find the right schools or step-down programs as they transition back home. The best educational consultants will also regularly follow up with the family and the school to monitor the child's progress in the therapeutic program, and they may even act as admission advocates for the children returning to traditional day schools if administrators have

misgivings about enrolling students who had to go through a therapeutic program in the first place. Our experience has been that many
private and parochial schools, and even some public high schools,
are hesitant to accept students who have been in residential therapeutic programs. Educational consultants work diligently to inform
and enlighten administrators and admissions officers about the scope
of residential therapeutic schools and the success rates of their programs, but parents need to be mindful that reentry into a traditional
school may not always be easy on the logistics side, never mind the
emotional adjustment.

Some day school and traditional boarding school administrators
are more likely to accept a "returning student" where the school offi-
cials know the family and their circumstances than to accept a new
student with no background or track record at the school. Parents may
want to ask about the possibility and terms of their child being read-
mitted to their old school and balance that option with the potential
trouble of returning to the old peer group and environment.

The educational consultant who works with Rebecca's family was
nothing short of phenomenal. She more than deserves her national
reputation of excellence. Her understanding of the different schools
and their therapeutic models, her rapport with our children, and her
ability to network and advocate for our children's needs in a wide variety of educational settings has been astonishing. Meeting and getting
to know her has been the silver lining in the ordeal of finding appropriate placements. Not every family is so lucky.

During a parents' workshop at a residential treatment facility in
Utah, one of the families lamented that their educational consultant
"took the money and ran" with no follow-up or additional help after
the initial placement was made. Educational consulting, much like
the therapeutic boarding school industry itself, is a new and still relatively unregulated industry.[23] As the researchers Reamer and Siegel
point out, "There is no educational consultant license, so consumers

have no assurance that their educational consultant has formal training in the fields of education, learning disabilities, adolescent development, counseling, or mental and behavioral health although advanced knowledge in all these areas is essential to adequately address a teen's needs and match them with appropriate programs."[24] However, the IECA is aggressive in monitoring the qualifications of its members, and every year the requirements become more stringent.

Caveat emptor. Screen your educational consultant as closely as you screen the programs you select for your children. The best referrals for a strong consultant will come from other parents, health care providers, and the educators working with your children. Remember, too, that the educational consultants work for you, not the schools. In their code of ethics, the IECA makes it clear that an educational consultant is never to accept money or other compensation from the schools or programs to which they make their referrals. Educational consultants do not have to be members of the IECA, but membership in the IECA for your consultant is much like a NATSAP affiliation for your school: those memberships and affiliations are another layer of insurance that you are dealing with qualified, ethical people.

To gain membership in the IECA, an individual must:

- Have completed at least a master's degree from an accredited college or university. Alternatively, an applicant may demonstrate comparable educational training or appropriate professional experience.
- Have completed at least three years of experience in counseling or admissions, with a minimum of one year of independent practice.
- Have advised at least fifty students while the candidate was employed in an institutional setting or working in private practice.
- Have conducted at least twenty-five "evaluative campus visits" to "troubled teen programs" within the last calendar year.

• Have professional references from at least two college or independent school admissions officers or psychologists/counselors with whom the candidate has worked in the admission process. The IECA also requires a third reference from a present IECA member, another educational professional, or a client family.

The IECA also has specialty designations for educational consultants qualified in Learning Disabilities (LD) and Special Needs (N). To earn either of those designations members must complete a separate application with additional requirements to demonstrate expertise in the respective fields. Requirements for IECA membership are demanding, and it can take several years for an IECA applicant to meet them. In spite of all the present demands for IECA membership, many people feel even more training is needed—including members of the IECA. Some clinicians feel that the IECA guidelines are "not nearly as rigorous, clearly defined, or specific as the typical licensing regulations for the prominent allied professions in mental health such as social work, psychology, marriage and family therapy, and counseling."[25] As the field grows and evolves, the need for professional certification becomes more likely. As a parent looking for a strong IEC, your best bet for finding one is to have strong referrals from several sources.

Over the past few years, the IECA administration and board have ramped up the efforts to implement stronger requirements for professional membership. As the Independent Educational Consultants Association evolves and matures, even more stringent guidelines will be put in place to ensure that clients receive the highest level of professionalism and expertise. With a solid referral and IECA membership, however, your educational consultant is an invaluable partner and advocate for your family. Our best counsel at this juncture is to try to not make a therapeutic school placement on your own. Most educational consultants will work with you across state lines via e-mail, phone, or Skype, so rarely is there a circumstance where you can't find an ethical, experienced consultant to help you.

Even after you've gone through the process of screening and hiring a qualified IEC, you'll need to keep four critical factors in mind as you select a therapeutic school:

1. *Avoid schools or programs that use a "boot camp" approach in dealing with troubled adolescents.* Strong evidence has been available for some time which clearly shows that harsh, shaming, labeling, or pejorative responses to teens can have a profoundly negative impact. These methodologies simply don't work.[26]

2. *Make certain the facility you choose for your child is managed by credentialed educators and licensed mental health specialists who follow best-practice protocols based on solid scientific evidence that has been documented in professional literature.* Likewise, you'll want to avoid schools and programs that are run by people who "rely primarily on ideology and beliefs which are unsupported by solid research evidence."[27]

   In later chapters we'll take a closer look at those specific programs and practices which parents and clinicians should NOT consider for their children or clients. NATSAP schools will all follow a best-practices protocol, and you can find additional information on a wide variety of therapeutic schools and their educational and treatment philosophies in *Woodbury Reports,* an annual publication compiled by educational consultant Lon Woodbury. Woodbury takes the written reports of the educational consultants who have visited the different schools to give a yearly update on the facilities, their staff, and their practices. You can access much of the information at the companion website for *Woodbury Reports:* www.strugglingteens.com.

3. *Make certain the program you choose is licensed by the appropriate state or federal agencies and that the academic division of the*

school is following state guidelines or secondary independent school guidelines and curriculum. For instance, residential treatment centers are often accredited by the Joint Commission. Joint Commission accreditation will nearly always be seen with hospital-based programs, addiction programs, and the more clinical models of RTCs as opposed to the residentially based models. Similarly, any wilderness education program you consider should be accredited by the Outdoor Behavioral Healthcare Industry Council (OBHIC), the National Association of Therapeutic Wilderness Camping (NATWC), and/or by NATSAP. To make the process even more complex and confusing, parents need to be aware that there are excellent, effective programs that aren't under the auspices of these regulatory agencies. Once again, your IEC is your best guide and counsel in these situations.

4. *Be certain the program you choose adequately addresses your child's and your family's needs with appropriate therapeutic approach and modality.* Ascertaining which therapeutic programs and approaches are going to work best for your child without professional help is going to be challenging to say the least. But if you find yourself in the position of having to make a decision without input from a qualified clinician or educational consultant, you can tap into two excellent research sources. The first is the Cochrane Library, a collection of databases (www.thecochranelibrary.com) and its subsidiary the Cochrane Reviews, which is a collection of hundreds of reports on the best mental health care interventions currently available. The Cochrane Reviews are written so that nonprofessionals can understand the research findings, and the Cochrane organization has extensive glossaries online. The second research source is the Campbell Collaboration (www.campbellcollaboration.org), which provides an online archive of *Campbell Systematic*

Reviews. These overviews are "designed to provide high quality evidence of 'what works' in the mental health arena."[28]

To simplify what can seem like an overwhelming endeavor, NATSAP has designed a checklist that IECs and parents can use to improve their odds of picking a safe, effective program:

- Verify licensure and accreditation of the facility. The NATSAP website provides a list of those accrediting agencies.
- Verify the licensure of the clinical and therapeutic staff.
- Verify that the academic curriculum is accredited by the state or a recognized academic accrediting body.
- If counseling is offered at the facility, find out if it is done by school employees, adjunct staff, or independent contractors.
- Obtain multiple independent sources of information about the school—not just from the school's website or staff.
- Talk to the students at the facility without the staff present.
- Inquire about clinical outcomes and how they are measured.
- Ask about program length and what factors determine readiness for completion.
- Ask about the program's philosophy of change and methods of discipline and restraint.
- Ask what's expected of families.
- Ask about restrictions on family communication and visitation.
- Ask for a description of program levels or stages of progress.
- Understand that the therapeutic school is just one step and just one piece of a collaborative effort to help your child.

chapter 6

Major Therapeutic and Treatment Models

*After Andy withdrew from school in Atlanta, I made an appoint-
ment with his psychiatrist for myself—not for a therapy session
or a medication check, but to get information. I knew something
serious was going on with Andy at this point, but I had no idea
what was happening inside his head. Being a stepparent put me
in a tenuous position, too. How much did I have the right to ask?
Even though Andy was living with us full-time, I knew I still had
to be cautious about boundaries and confidentiality. Andy's doctor
told me what she could:*

*"Before age eighteen we don't want to put a formal diagnosis
on what these kids are going through. The personality and sense
of self are still developing, you understand. But right now, I'd say
Andy has some characteristics of borderline personality disorder."*

*I didn't understand what she was talking about. "A personality
disorder?" I said. "Which one?" I didn't realize at the time that
borderline personality disorder was the description; I'd never heard
of it. I called my husband and Andy's mom after my meeting with
the psychiatrist. Andy's dad is a physician; his mom is a registered
nurse, and my background is in speech pathology, but none of us
knew the first thing about the condition Andy's doctor was suggest-*

ing. We learned fast, though. It was a steep and painful learning curve. We read everything we could find on the disorder, discovering how serious a problem it is, but also finding how new therapeutic approaches were bringing strong, positive results for adults who had been diagnosed with the disease. We had some hope. —R. H.

AS YOU TALK with clinicians and read through parent handbooks from the different therapeutic schools, you'll run into a new and strange vocabulary. Unless you have a background in psychology, the terminology used to describe the major therapeutic and treatment models utilized by the schools and RTCs may seem like a foreign language. Our goal in this chapter is to give you a brief, user-friendly definition of the most common clinical approaches and also a description of how these therapeutic modalities are used. Some of these philosophies and approaches merit a set of textbooks and graduate level classes to fully describe, but if you want more in-depth information on a particular treatment approach, the counselors at your child's school can steer you toward more material, or you may use our reference sources as a springboard for your own research.

PSYCHOTHERAPY APPROACHES

Basically the field of psychotherapy today can be divided into four major camps which differ significantly in philosophical approach and also in the design and delivery of the treatment methods. Proponents of each camp love to debate the others about the superiority of their stance, and you may find members of one group in the opposite corner of the room from their colleagues from another camp at professional meetings and holiday parties! All debate aside, though, each approach has merit and efficacy when used by skillful clinicians with the right clients.

The first group is known as the *psychoanalytical* or *psychodynamic* camp. Based on the pioneering work of Sigmund Freud, Carl Jung, and others, this approach examines the early childhood experiences of the individual in treatment and gives special consideration to the role of the subconscious mind and how early experience and the subconscious work to affect the person's feelings, behaviors, and thoughts. The goal of treatment is to bring the client to a place of insight and self-awareness about why they feel and act as they do and to use that insight to lead them to healing and healthier choices and actions.

On the other side of the room you'll find the *behavioral* camp. The behaviorists tend to focus on eliminating or reducing unhealthy behaviors and substitute healthier, more positive alternatives. This change is brought about through operant conditioning, which is a system of rewards for the desired behaviors, and counterconditioning, where a client is gradually exposed and desensitized to negative triggers. For example, think of a person who is afraid of dogs. This person would begin his therapeutic work by petting a gentle puppy and gradually work his way up to petting the neighbor's golden retriever.

Closely related to the behavioral approach is the third camp, *cognitive therapy.* Using this method, clinicians help troubled individuals recognize and adjust distorted thinking patterns. The goal of this approach is also to help clients assess and react to situations in a healthier way. Through recording and analyzing the client's feelings and reactions in a series of daily events, the therapist can guide the individual to more logical thoughts and conclusions.

In the fourth camp are the clinicians who utilize the *humanistic* approach, which strives to help clients realize their full potential as individuals. The therapists using this approach actively listen to their clients and stay nonjudgmental and supportive as their clients seek to be authentic in expressing their feelings. In this environment of acceptance the client's self-esteem will hopefully increase, enabling the individual to make healthier choices and have stronger relationships.[29]

Obviously, this is a fairly simplistic explanation of four complex and evolving approaches to psychology, but now as you read the specific types of therapeutic delivery systems that the schools and RTCs will use with your child, you can tell which of the main philosophies they follow, and you'll see that many of these methods are hybrids, drawing on features from more than one of the major fields. Also, programs offer a combination of models in group or individual therapy, and as your child progresses in his or her treatment, the delivery system may shift somewhat.

Cognitive Behavioral Therapy (CBT)

As the name suggests, this approach is a blending of behavioral and cognitive methods in which the students are given specific exercises and guidance for correcting distorted thinking about themselves and others. At the same time, they'll be gradually shaping maladaptive behaviors into healthier, more constructive patterns.[30]

Dialectical Behavioral Therapy (DBT)

Dialectical behavioral therapy is a specialized form of cognitive behavioral therapy developed by Dr. Marsha M. Linehan and her colleagues at the University of Washington. DBT incorporates a client evaluation of his or her own distortions of thought along with the implementation or meditation and mindfulness with the overall goal of reducing anxiety and providing the client with a "skill set" to use in coping with and diffusing maladaptive, destructive thoughts and behaviors.

Milieu Therapy

This approach uses a structured group setting in which the students can learn healthier patterns of behavior through the modeling and support of their peers and the counselors. While milieu therapy takes some time to affect the needed changes, it gradually builds a safe and trusting environment for the students in which they feel more comfortable initiating changes in behavior without fear of being judged. Milieu therapy seeks to build a sense of empathy and community, but with clear-cut expectations on the students' responsibility and accountability.[31]

Positive Peer Culture

This therapeutic method developed by Harry Vorrath at the University of Kentucky is a "unified, cohesive social system in which both students and staff are devoted to responsible, lawful behavior." Open, honest communication is shown to be more productive than confrontation, and students begin to see their peer group as the primary source of help and support as they let go of destructive patterns and embrace change. Peer respect and acceptance become the change agents. As researcher William Wasmund writes, "People do not resist changing, they resist *being changed.*"[32]

Strengths-Based Programming

In this model the therapist and his or her client discuss the areas in which the student needs or wants to make changes. Afterwards, they make a list of the student's emotional and cognitive strengths and outline how they're going to use these strengths to facilitate the targeted change areas. As goals are realized, many weaknesses are transformed into strengths, and the student is guided into a pattern of continual empowerment and healing.[33]

Person-Centered Therapy (PCT)

This approach, originally developed by Carl Rogers in the 1940s and '50s, uses a humanistic model. Therapists strive to create a safe, non-judgmental environment for the students by consistently providing empathy and unconditional positive regard for them. The goal is to help the students find their own solutions to problems and destructive behaviors. In this approach, the trust level and empathy between the student and his or her counselor is especially crucial for success.[34]

Equine-Assisted Therapy

In this relatively brief and intensive therapy model, the powerful and dynamic horse is introduced into the treatment program. The student participates in riding and training activities with the horses and later discusses the feelings, behaviors, and patterns that went along with the activities. Equine-assisted psychotherapy (EAP) enhances the nonverbal communication skills of the students as well as their assertiveness, creative problem-solving, and overall confidence. Equine-assisted learning (EAL) is similar to EAP, but with assisted learning, the focus is on helping the students meet educational goals instead of emotional ones.[35]

a. The nonprofit professional association for Equine Assisted Psychotherapy and Learning services (EAGALA) oversees the training for clinicians and equine handlers utilizing the equine-assisted psychotherapy (EAP) and equine-assisted learning (EAL) programs and also strives to raise public awareness about the success of these programs, as well as helping individuals and schools obtain funding to implement the treatment model.[36]

b. *The Trails Program*, or T.R.A.I.L.S. (Therapeutic Riding Assists Individual Learning Skills), is another popular equine therapy program which stresses not only the emotional benefits of riding, but also the three-dimensional, rhythmic motion of the horse's gait. The sensory input of a horse's gait to the rider is similar to the human gait, and this therapeutic approach is commonly used with children with physical disabilities as well as students working through emotional and cognitive problems.[37]

Addiction Therapy Models

Recovery from drug and/or alcohol addiction involves, of course, much more than the initial detoxification stage. Getting clean and sober is challenging; staying clean and sober even more so. Today the National Institute on Drug Abuse (NIDA) recommends detoxification be followed up with counseling, relapse prevention programs, and medication when indicated.[38] Numerous counseling and relapse prevention programs are in use, and they can pull from all of the major psychology approaches. For our purposes, we'll look at three of the most commonly used models for students in therapeutic schools.

The Twelve-Step Model

This therapeutic approach was first used in the 1930s by the organizers of Alcoholics Anonymous (AA) as a method of recovery from alcoholism. The method has been adapted successfully for many types of addiction problems from cocaine use to gambling to compulsive eating. The American Psychological Association sums up the Twelve-Step Program as: admitting that one cannot control the addiction or compulsion, and recognizing that a higher, spiritual power is needed to overcome the problem. Additionally, the recovering addict must examine the past mistakes they've made with the help of an experienced sponsor and try to make amends for these past mistakes. The recovering addict then begins to live a new life with a new code of behavior and strives to help others who are suffering from the same addictions or compulsions.[39]

The Seven Challenges Model

The Seven Challenges treatment model differs from the traditional AA Twelve-Step Program in that it was developed specifically for adolescents. Dr. Robert Schwebel initiated development of this program in 1991 with a group of teenagers in a residential facility in Tucson, Arizona. From the onset, Schwebel wanted the program to be developmentally appropriate for the age group, and he also designed the program to be culturally sensitive and to address issues that often accompany addiction problems.[40]

SMART Recovery (Self Management and Recovery Training)

Initiated in the early 1990s, this approach combines therapeutic techniques from motivational enhancement therapy and cognitive behavioral therapy. The program focuses on four major points in the recovery process: building the students' motivation, helping them cope with urges, enhancing problem solving, and balancing lifestyle choices. A more secular approach than the Twelve Steps of AA, SMART Recovery is sometimes used as an alternative or a supplement to Twelve Steps.[41]

OTHER MODELS

Native American Mythology

Native American mythology uses the long recognized impact of traditional myth and storytelling on the human experience. By participating in Native American cultural rituals and understanding the symbols and allegory of the mythical stories, clinicians employing this therapeutic approach seek to help clients understand their own life problems, challenges, and transitions as part of a universal struggle in the journey of mankind.[42]

The Hero's Journey

Outlined in Joseph Campbell's book *The Hero with a Thousand Faces*, the hero's journey incorporates elements of Native American mythology as well. Within this Jungian healing approach, the client is guided from the initial stage of departure and separation where he or she first reaches out for help through descent, initiation, and penetration. In this second step of therapy, the counselor and student work together closely to examine the conscious and unconscious elements of feelings and actions as they apply to the client's life situation. The process culminates with "return" where the client emerges from the experience stronger, more integrated, and living a healthier life with stronger relationships.[43]

Eye Movement Desensitization and Reprocessing (EMDR)

Developed by psychologist Francine Shapiro, this form of psychotherapy is especially effective in treating both adults and adolescents who have suffered from abuse or trauma. EMDR is one of the preferred methods for helping individuals with post-traumatic stress disorder (PTSD). According to Shapiro's theory, repeated or especially distressing events (such as rape or military combat) can overwhelm the usual cognitive and neurological coping mechanisms. The experience and memory of the event aren't adequately resolved, and the experience is stored in an isolated memory network in the brain.

The actual process of EMDR is fairly complex and involved, but here is the basic description of how it's done: utilizing a photograph that represents the disturbing event along with the negative thoughts and body sensations associated with the trauma, the therapist asks his or her client to follow a moving object for about fifteen to thirty seconds. Additionally, auditory tones, hand-tapping, or other stimuli are added to this process of alternating attention between the moving object and the personal association.

After the process, the client is asked to rate his or her level of positive cognition as well as their level of distress. With repeated exposure to the coupled stress and eye movement followed by feedback and introspection, the distress levels gradually fall. It's a physiological approach to a psychological challenge, and the research shows it's extremely effective.[44]

These are some of the most widely used therapeutic approaches you'll see utilized in treatment centers and schools, but there are many, many more you could encounter. Remember, you'll often see combinations of therapeutic approaches or changes in the modalities used as your child progresses through his or her work.

chapter 7

Adjustment and Negotiation

After three months of treatment in Montana, Andy said to us, "No matter how hard you try, no matter how sympathetic you want to be, you can't imagine for a second what it's like for me here. It insults me for you to even say that you get it. You don't get it. You're at home with your friends and your life . . . sleeping in your own bed. I'm in this place alone. It's horrible, and all I want to do is come home."

Our hearts broke all over again about the choice we had to make to send him away for treatment. It was clear that Andy needed the intensive therapeutic work of residential treatment; it was clear he needed a level of help that we couldn't give him at home; but everything Andy said about his homesickness was true. Few of us can appreciate how tough it is to leave home against our will—to be in a place where we don't know anyone and don't know who to believe or who to trust. It would be a harrowing experience for any healthy adult, let alone for an adolescent struggling with emotional problems, substance abuse, or learning issues. The closest analogy I can find is a soldier leaving—maybe not for combat, but certainly for something as grueling as basic training.

—R. H.

IN ALMOST ALL of the professional literature and the materials presented at parenting workshops at different schools, a clear message comes through: *Things are going to get worse before they get better—not only for your child, but for your entire family.* Even if your child acknowledges that she needs help in the early stages of a program (which is unusual), you can count on the fact that she is going to be miserable, homesick, and willing and able to use every tool in her psychological hardware store to get you to bring her home. And can you blame her? Wouldn't you do the same if you were in her shoes? In some cases the children are openly manipulating; in some cases it's unconscious. The underlying motivation isn't as important as the fact that your son or daughter is earnestly upset, frightened, and out of balance. All we can do as parents at this stage is actively listen, validate that their fears are legitimate, and acknowledge how difficult this experience of being away must be for our children. It's also important to admit that we can't fully understand the pain they're feeling even though we know it's overwhelming for them. And in that admission lies the paradox that begins healing: Our sons and daughters are individuals unique from us, our children certainly, but their identity and sense of self stands apart. They own their feelings and are ultimately responsible for their personal decisions and choices unless they have a serious, underlying mental illness. The purpose of the therapeutic environment is to give them the skills they need to function better emotionally and educationally, and to give them a safe place to practice those skills before they transition home.

The old cliché "easier said than done" applies perfectly here. Especially in the first few weeks and months that your child is away, you can count on nearly every letter and phone call being emotionally charged with requests of *"Get me out of here!"* Our children will deny they had significant problems in the first place, they'll swear that whatever actions or behaviors got them into trouble initially are now totally behind them, and they'll promise that they'll never be in trouble again. They'll tell us that they don't belong in this place, and they'll try to convince us that the other students have problems much more serious than theirs. They'll tell us that the staff is abusing them or neglecting them—that they're being starved and beaten, that they're not being given their medications or are being given too much of something not prescribed for them in the first place. They may try to convince us that they've been placed in a gulag, not an emotional-growth boarding school. They may try to run away.

Now comes the hard part. You have to trust the staff and the program with the health and safety of your child. Do not pick up and bring home your son or daughter too soon. Do not terminate the program or "rescue" your child. Even if on the surface your son or daughter seems more grounded and emotionally stronger, remember that significant changes take time and reinforcement. You have to let the program do its work, and your child will need to fully internalize the changes, not simply check the boxes. Guilt, doubt, and second-guessing are going to nag you constantly. So are the judgments and well-meaning (but typically misinformed) advice of your friends and extended family. Hold fast. Remember the course of events and choices that got your family to this point in the first place.

Once your children realize that you're committed to seeing the program through to completion and that you're not going to pull them out, they're much more likely to settle in to the routine of school life and engage in the therapeutic work they need to do. This acceptance is a messy process, however. You may have several weeks where your child seems to be adjusting well and accepting the program only to be followed by a setback where he or she is once again raging at you or begging you to bring him or her home. Change, even good change, provokes stress, and as your child and family grow and heal, you'll feel the effects of that stress constantly.

Just as we can't completely grasp what our children are experiencing in the therapeutic environment, neither can they understand what we're going through at home or what their siblings are feeling. Sarah was devastated when her brother had to leave, and she mistakenly interpreted the cleaning out a closet of clothes that Andy had long out-grown as a gesture of "throwing Andy out" or "giving Andy away." She sobbed when she left her brother's room, and there was no consoling her. Likewise, Rebecca's husband berated himself constantly, wonder-ing what he had done wrong as a parent. He had to fight a depression and anxiety every bit as real and fearful as some of the emotions Andy faced.

Intellectually we may know that we've done everything humanly possible to help our children, but what we know in our heads doesn't always match up to what we feel in our hearts when we are worried about our children's health and well-being. The whole family dynamic changes when a child leaves home for treatment, and, once again, change invokes stress. Schedules are different, mealtimes are different, and holidays and special occasions seem strange and lonely without our children present.

And finally, there is the honest admission of relief that makes us feel guilty too. Whatever problems the child was experiencing—substance abuse, mental illness, legal issues—are at arm's length for a short while. They are out of the house, at least to some degree, along with our child. Of course we feel relieved. Perhaps we're not on suicide watch anymore; we can exhale. Or perhaps we don't have to worry about the police showing up at the door with an arrest warrant or the crushing news of an accident. *We feel relief, and we may feel embarrassed or unloving because we're experiencing that relief.* For the first time, per-haps in a long time, we can attend to our marriage, our other children, our work, ourselves.

Your family will go through a grief process similar in many ways to the grief families experience after a death. The hopes and aspirations you had for your child may be radically changed or diminished. Some of the initial dreams you had for your child may be dead, at least in the short term. But your child is alive. Your family will not face an easy road, and nothing can hurry the healing process or take away the sense of loss, but you have every reason for hope. And that hope and your faith should be important guy-wires you can grasp for support along this journey.

The typical length of stay at most residential therapeutic programs is twelve to twenty-four months, and as you try to calculate the time your child will be away, you'll also need to consider the time he or she will spend in wilderness or possibly a step-down program before transitioning home.

Andy's and Sarah's schools didn't give strict timelines on when the program would be completed. Instead, they gave parents and students a range of time and also clearly outlined the different steps in the process that the children and their families needed to complete before the program was finished. Achieving those steps and intermediate goals served to give the adolescents a stronger sense of accomplishment and mastery, and making their way up the therapeutic ladder usually meant greater freedom and more privileges at the school. It also won them the respect of younger, less experienced students and gave many of the teenaged "veterans" a chance to mentor younger students and serve in leadership roles.

One question, however, needs significantly more research and exploration: How long is *too* long in a residential program? That's a difficult question to answer. Obviously, it's going to vary with the child and his or her individual circumstances, and complex mental health and learning issues complicate matters. Ideally, the children or adolescents will get the help they need in as short a time as possible and then transition home to continue their development and growth with their families. The most important factor is giving the therapeutic process a chance to work and allowing healthy changes to take root, no matter what the time frame.

How much help can families reasonably expect from a therapeutic program? How much change and improvement will be long-lasting? There are dozens of success stories out there about children and families in different therapeutic environments, but it is important and ultimately much more compassionate to be honest and temper hope with realism. Some of the learning disabilities and cognitive problems these children face are going to be with them for the rest of their lives, and those challenges will most likely outlive parents and even siblings. In many instances families are going to need to have tough conversations with siblings and other relatives, and often thoughtful planning with financial and legal advisors is going to be necessary to protect and provide for many of these children when the parents no longer can. Advances in medications and therapeutic techniques also provide new hope for children with significant mental illness and emotional problems, but the fact remains that some of our children won't get much better, and they'll need significant psychiatric help and counseling for the rest of their lives. The same can be said for the children with substance abuse issues; we will all have to be vigilant—one day at a time.

The work of therapeutic schools and residential treatment centers does not provide a cure. Instead, the success of such programs lies in giving children and their families the skills and resources they need to cope with whatever issues they face and a safe place to practice and integrate those skills. It's a springboard for the rest of the adolescent's life. We're going to be required to reset the thermostat on our initial plans for our teenagers.

We have to be patient and give the programs time to work, and we as parents and family have our own share of "transformational work" to do while our children are away. It's critical to be invested in the therapeutic changes that will affect us all as our children transition home. The long-term research shows that families who are willing to partner in a school's programs and goals significantly increase their child's odds for success when he or she returns home.[45]

chapter 8

The Use of Psychotropic Medications in Therapeutic Boarding School Environments

The more we read about Andy's possible diagnosis, the more we realized that medications weren't going to be a quick, easy fix for the issues he was wrestling with. Some mental health conditions respond beautifully to psychotropic or other types of drugs combined with therapy, but borderline personality disorder isn't one of them. But Andy was taking medications to help with the underlying depression and anxiety that go along with the disorder. It was always a dance. We were constantly trying to keep the medications at the right level to give Andy some relief from the psychic pain he endured, but we didn't want to overmedicate him and put him in a stupor, either. We also knew he was growing so fast that keeping the medications at the right level was going to be even trickier. —R. H.

AT A 2009 parents' orientation program at a residential treatment center near Knoxville, Tennessee, Dr. Reggie Raman, the staff psychiatrist, gave a clear and hopeful explanation of how the RTC model helps in the medical assessment of struggling adolescents and how these more thorough and accurate assessments make prescribing appropriate types of medications at the appropriate levels easier.

"Before, when I was working in a traditional psychiatric hospital setting with adolescents," he said, "I would typically see them on the unit for just a few days. Federal and state laws and the cost constraints of managed care wouldn't let us keep children too long. In the short time that I saw these young people, they were in crisis, and our goal was to get the children stabilized as best we could and get them ready for release. I couldn't observe them closely for any significant period of time, and it was sometimes difficult to get a good picture of how they were functioning day to day and what types of medications and what levels were going to be optimal. We did all we could based on the information and history we had, but unfortunately, as is so often the case with short-term hospitalizations, we would release the children to the same problems and environments that had gotten them to the hospital in the first place. Not surprisingly, many of them ended up in the hospital again."

He went on, "Seeing a child in a residential treatment center gives me the luxury of time. I can watch a child over a period of weeks or months in social and academic settings. I can get sustained input from their teachers and counselors. I get a much better picture of what the efficacy of a medication is or will likely be for the student, and I can monitor their progress. Often, I can titrate a child's dosage of medications down or even take the children off certain drugs completely."[46]

A former academic advisor at Island View, a residential treatment center just outside Salt Lake City, echoed Raman's thoughts: "Our goal is to have the students function as well as possible with as little medication as possible. Whenever it's realistic, we'd like to see the students off medications completely, although we realize that's not often feasible, and we respect the fact that certain drugs help many of our students enormously."[47] All clinicians agree that having a student arrive at school or a residential treatment center with a "cocktail" blend of medications is disheartening, and that situation makes the job of the treatment facility much more difficult.

Most of us know from early experience with our children's therapeutic work that medications are just one weapon in the arsenal we need to help our kids. Seldom, if ever, is there a situation where a physician can simply prescribe a capsule or tablet to solve a mental health or behavioral problem. The issues are too complex. Some medications will provide symptom reduction for our children, while other drugs for certain disorders will actually help address the underlying organic cause. Hopefully, our children will get help on both fronts, but we have to acknowledge that even in the hands of the most adept clinicians, the type and dosage of medications our children receive is often a matter of trial and error before a physician and treatment team can find which regimen is going to have the greatest efficacy.

Naturally, you'll want to make sure your child's medications are being properly monitored by an experienced psychiatrist while your son or daughter is enrolled in a therapeutic school, and you'll also want to be certain that the medications are being dispensed and taken correctly at the school. "Cheeking," swapping, and bartering medications is commonplace for students in therapeutic environments, just as it is in ordinary school settings, and the medical and administrative staffs have to stay alert and observant to prevent it from happening.

In summary, psychotropic medications can be an extremely effective and useful tool in your child's treatment, but they're only one tool, and they have to be used along with therapy and a healthy environment for optimal results.

chapter 9

Making the Grade: Ensuring Academic and Emotional Progress for Your Child

"The school work here is pretty shoddy. They just give us these packets to work on—all these worksheets we have to fill out. And we can ask questions if we need to, but most of the time I don't. I just fill them out and turn them in. I don't think I'm really learning much. But in Utah? Yeah, those teachers were really good—especially my English teacher. We had all these papers we had to do. The work there was much tougher; it was almost as hard as what I had back in school in Atlanta."

—Andy describing the schoolwork at his RTC in Tennessee

THE ACADEMIC RIGOR of therapeutic schools, as we have mentioned before, varies greatly. Some programs offer challenging college preparatory classes and opportunities for the students to add Advanced Placement (AP) or other enrichment programs, while other schools will offer special classes and teaching techniques to help address the needs of students with learning disabilities. Still other programs will provide basic, standard curricula that allow students to catch up or reinforce academic areas where they may have fallen behind. And many programs offer a combination of options. Working with your educational consultant and talking directly with the educational staff at the school will help you decide whether or not the program is going to be a good match for your child's educational needs. Sarah's school in North Carolina helped arrange an independent study for her in a foreign language that the school didn't offer, and the school's principal went out of his way to help find a local tutor and an appropriate curriculum. A student's specific academic needs can't always be addressed in this way, obviously, but it doesn't hurt to ask, and if you're willing to help do the legwork to set up an enrichment program for your son or daughter, many programs will try to accommodate a reasonable request.

Academic schedules also vary widely from school to school. At one therapeutic school in New England, the ninth- through twelfth-graders follow a routine Monday-to-Friday block schedule, and they also have classes on Saturday. At the other end of the spectrum, some schools have classes for only half a day, and the grading periods are much shorter than the ones in traditional day schools or boarding schools. Typically classes are much smaller in therapeutic programs than they are in ordinary schools, and there is nearly always a set time in the late afternoon or evenings for study hall and extra help. Smaller class sizes with more individualized attention, paired with a structured homework time, is often a huge bonus for struggling teenagers. The distractions of Facebook, cell phones, and video games are gone, providing the students with a quiet place to concentrate.

When your child first enrolls at a therapeutic school, the academic staff and/or your educational consultant will meet with you and have you sign the necessary releases so that they can review your child's previous testing and academic transcripts. Likewise, when your child is ready to come home, you'll once again meet with the academic team to develop an educational transition plan for your child and help you through the paperwork gauntlet of getting the right forms to the right people.

Just as in a traditional day school, you'll be scheduled for parent-teacher conferences over the phone and face-to-face when you come for campus visits or workshops at the therapeutic facility. You'll also get grades and educational updates every three to six weeks (or more often if problems arise or the situation warrants more communication). Parent handbooks will usually have clear-cut instructions about who to contact at the school if you have questions or concerns about academic issues. If your child has special educational needs that require an IEP or 504 Plan, you'll be given regular updates on your child's progress toward goals and will be notified when new goals are set. The teachers are considered an important part of the treatment team working with your child. Their input and observations are as valuable as the work of the counselors, physicians, and house staff.

Not surprisingly, many therapeutic schools will continue academic classes throughout the summer to give students more structure and continuity. But you may also find that your child's school takes a break of a week or longer between academic sessions or study units— not only in the summer but also through the entire year. While the emotional-growth or therapeutic school may not call your student a "freshman" or a "sophomore," you'll be able to determine exactly when your child is earning the unit credits he or she needs for high school graduation and college entrance from the reports the school sends you.

Many educational consultants feel that, in many instances, the academic standards of therapeutic programs are not up to par. Often, students are given packets of materials in various subjects and are expected to complete the work in these packets with the help and oversight of their teachers. For college-bound students, this method of learning isn't rigorous enough and doesn't give the student the writing, critical thinking, or higher-level mathematics experience they'll need to be successful in a university setting. There is a strong movement on the part of educational consultants to broaden and improve the academic programs at therapeutic schools.

Gauging emotional and therapeutic progress isn't as clear-cut as evaluating the work needed for a unit credit of biology or American history, unfortunately. Yet parents and students need some sort of yardstick by which to measure the advances they're making. Most NATSAP-affiliated schools will have a series of accomplishment steps or stages that are clearly explained to the parents when their teenagers enroll. As mentioned before, working through these steps or completing the therapeutic goals associated with the stages will earn the adolescent different "ranks" or levels of freedom, privileges, and trust from the staff. More importantly, the students should be gaining a sense of mastery and confidence as they move through their program toward the ultimate goal of going home with stronger coping skills and resilience. The outward praise and rewards are important, but the most critical progress takes place when the child internalizes the accomplishments and finds a sense of integrity from within.

One of the Aspen Education Group's schools for middle school-aged girls labeled their stages as Sun, Moon, and Star to mark the progress students made to sets of progressively more challenging therapeutic goals. Likewise, Andy's school called their stages Mouse, Buffalo, Bear, and Eagle to designate how far the young men had come in the program. No matter what the label, levels follow a commonly accepted time frame and transition. The first four months of the program are typically seen as a period of adjustment and negotiation where the student comes to terms with being away from home in the first place and following the treatment guidelines. Dr. Paul Case calls this initial phase "handing them over."[48]

The next four to eight months encompass the heart of the therapeutic work, where new behaviors and coping skills are introduced to the students and reinforced. At the end of this phase, the child's discharge plan is outlined for the first time, while the counselors and support staff continue to reinforce and affirm the child's healthier, more productive actions and attitudes. At this point, the treatment team (counselors, therapists, teachers, physicians, and support staff) will also tackle the more difficult, deeply ingrained problems that the student has exhibited. All the while the student is working, the family should be working too, on their own individual and group counseling. The whole family system must grow and heal; the child cannot do it alone. Discharge preparation usually takes two to four months, and once the adolescent is back at home, the follow-up portion of the program will last up to a year.[49]

At this point, it's important for families to remind themselves that the therapeutic schools and residential programs don't provide a "cure" and that the teenagers have not been "fixed." Instead, the programs have hopefully provided the students and their families with a healthier, more effective set of coping skills that they can use as a base as they reenter mainstream life.

chapter 10

Oversight and Regulation in the Therapeutic Boarding School Industry

We had tremendous respect for the clinical director at Andy's RTC in Tennessee, and we thought his therapist was one of the most insightful, effective counselors we met, but the real hero, the person who had the greatest impact on Andy's daily life, was a houseparent named Mr. Jones. While some of the other staff looked the other way when Andy was being taunted or bullied by other students, Mr. Jones advocated for Andy. He did his best to make sure that the more aggressive students didn't abuse Andy and other vulnerable kids. He was also a sounding board for Andy. Mr. Jones would listen when Andy felt the other staff members weren't doing enough to stop the teasing and cruelty. When Andy finished the program in Tennessee, it was Mr. Jones he wanted most at his exit conference. Years later, Andy still keeps in touch with Mr. Jones, and he burns CDs for him at Christmas. Never underestimate how important the houseparents are to your child's treatment and healing. —R. H.

THERAPEUTIC BOARDING SCHOOLS and residential care facilities are not without their detractors, and even the most cursory Internet search of the industry will bring you to dozens of articles from psychologists and children's advocacy groups who believe that the whole industry should be shut down. They claim that the environments are contrived and unnatural and that the child's separation from his or her family and friends is detrimental. And of course, the most alarming statements are the reports about facilities that don't take adequate care of the children's basic health and educational needs. The critics give chilling descriptions of schools where the use of medications is unmonitored or abused and situations where the children are subject to emotional and physical abuse. Although rare, those situations of abuse do exist, and what individual is more vulnerable to abuse than a troubled adolescent who cannot readily leave the school compound or communicate freely with his or her parents? We need to have an extremely high level of trust with a school and have that trust validated constantly if we're going to turn our children over to them for treatment.

Beyond checking for NATSAP affiliation, secondary school accreditation, and the referrals of educational consultants, what can we as parents and educators do to ensure the safety of our children while they're enrolled in an emotional-growth school or RTC?

Obviously, when you visit the school you'll want to check for cleanliness, not just in the common areas and the classrooms, but also in the dorms, the bathrooms, and the kitchens. Be very leery of any facility that won't let you have a thorough view of all these places. Have a meal on campus if at all possible, and if you can, eat with the students and talk with them about the teachers, the therapists, and the program itself. Once again, any school that tries to censor your conversations with its students is suspect. The only exception to this rule is treatment centers that are working with adolescents who are violent or exhibiting psychotic behavior. Your educational consultant and referring physician can help you navigate the difficult path you'll need to take to get objective feedback on these programs.

On the initial visit to Andy's school in Montana, Rebecca and her husband got a full tour of the campus from two of the older students who were due to complete their program and return home in a few weeks. They talked openly about the problems they had faced, how tough the adjustment had been in the first few weeks they were away from home, and what the program in Montana had done for them as well as issues they were still working through. They were brutally honest about the staff and teachers; some were beloved, some were the butt of jokes, but it was the candor and transparency of their comments that were the most reassuring. No staff member was shadowing to overhear what the students had to say.

Look at the overall health and hygiene of the students themselves. Are their clothes clean? Their hair? Their faces? Their nails? Look closely. Sarah is a vegetarian, and to hear her tell the story, her evening meal at school was often nothing more than a cup of gruel and a crust of stale bread—but her healthy weight and glowing skin showed that her nutrition was more than adequate. As you look around the facility, check to see if the children have access to fruit or other healthy snacks during the day. Some schools limit the students' access to caffeine and processed sugar (a policy that could serve us all well), but at Andy's and Sarah's schools, water, milk, and decaffeinated teas were almost always available.

The longer you can stay on campus—within reason, of course—for your visit and tour, the better. It's especially important to see how medications are distributed during and after meals and in the evenings before the teenagers go to bed. How closely does the staff check to make sure the students are compliant with their medicines? Is there a nurse on campus? How accessible is a board-certified psychiatrist who can monitor how well your child is doing on medications and adjust the dosage or type of drug if needed? Ask all these questions. Write down all the questions you have before your tour, and don't hesitate to call back and ask the staff and administrators follow-up questions if you have them. The school's willingness to share information is a strong indicator of how clearly they'll communicate with your family once your child is enrolled.

A clean campus with good meals and a well-equipped science lab are important, but the heart and soul of a program lies in the strength and competence of its staff. Two important markers of a program's effectiveness are the average educational levels of the staff and the average tenure of the school's therapists and teachers. Too many inexperienced counselors without at least a master's level education and heavy turnover are reasons for concern. The effectiveness of a program can change for the better or worse very quickly with administration or staff turnover, and parents may not always be immediately aware of these personnel changes. Once again, a strong educational consultant is invaluable at this point. He or she will have access to turnover information and staff credentials that would be nearly impossible for parents to ferret out in their own research. If your educational consultant can visit your child's program while your son or daughter is enrolled, you'll have validation that the facility is still using a solid, best practices approach.

In Montana, many of the peer leaders working with Andy and the other students had only completed their bachelor's degrees in psychology, social work, or special education, but almost without exception they were working toward their master's degrees or doctorates, and they had additional experience as educators or wilderness leaders.

Visit the classrooms if you can, the labs, the gyms. Talk to as many of the teachers as you practically can. If possible, sit in on part of an actual class and watch how the students interact with the teachers and each other in the classroom setting. How engaged are they? How challenging is the material, and how flexible are the instructors and the curriculum when the students need enrichment or remediation in a subject?

Ask about the types of therapeutic approaches the counselors use, and read and educate yourself as much as possible about the different treatment modalities that might be effective for your child. One size definitely does not fit all. Be honest with yourself about the limitations of self-education regarding complex behavioral and psychological issues, however. Don't be afraid to challenge the staff and counselors with your questions, but also respect the education and experience they have.

Another area to investigate as you tour schools is the student population itself. How serious are the problems the children are facing? Are these learned behavioral issues for the most part, or are things more serious? Are some of the students dealing with problems vastly different or more deeply entrenched than what your child is facing? Do their issues seem to be in line with the issues your child is facing? As parents, we have the natural tendency to think that our children's problems aren't as severe as those of others in the program. But we have to be realistic. It's true that an adolescent who is simply experimenting with marijuana has no business being in a program with an adolescent who has had a psychotic break, but it is equally true that a teenager who is suicidal could benefit from the same program as another student who has been sexually promiscuous. Acting "in" is as clinically significant as acting "out."

Your educational consultant will know the programs and the student population, and he or she can help you choose the most appropriate setting for your son or daughter. Has violence been an issue with any of the students at the school, and what protocols does the school have in place to deal with those types of problems should they arise? What happens if an adolescent demonstrates more serious educational or behavioral issues than before? What happens if your child or others severely regress in their treatment? Granted, these are tough, sensitive questions that you'll want to address discreetly with the program director and not at lunch with the history teacher.

How restricted is the movement of the students? In other words, can the students walk around campus between buildings or to and from activities and classes without staff supervision, or do they use a buddy system where the teenagers have to be in groups of two or more? In many facilities, independent time is a privilege the students earn by demonstrating responsibility and accountability for extended periods.

How closely supervised are the children in their dorms, during study time, and even in the bathrooms? It may seem an outlandish question to ask, but depending on the severity of your child's problems and his or her past behavior, you'll need to know how closely he or she will be monitored in different activities.

The demographics of the school population, while not a decisive factor, are an interesting consideration when you choose a school. In Montana nearly all the teenagers were from large urban areas on the West Coast, with a smaller number of students from Chicago, New York, Atlanta, Miami, and Denver. This was as sophisticated and cosmopolitan a crowd (for better and for worse) as you'll ever see in a group of high schoolers. As a rule, they were socially liberal and tolerant. One of them was a sixteen-year-old from Los Angeles who proudly announced that he had been clean and sober for eight months. He asked intelligent, insightful questions, sounding more like a forty-year-old man than a recovering teenager.

Andy eventually left the program in Montana to finish his work at a facility closer to home on the East Coast. The staff and counselors at this facility were every bit as dedicated and professional as the Montana team, but the student body was quite different. Most of the children at the latter facility were from smaller towns and cities in the Southeast. Their life experiences were different, their overall level of sophistication was different, and they tended to be more conservative politically and socially than their counterparts in Montana. This difference was neither inherently good nor bad, but it did prove a challenging point of adjustment for Andy, who had grown accustomed to the big-city viewpoints of his Montana peers.

Another issue to consider is how the treatment teams deal with conflict resolution between students. Once again, the systems in Montana and on the East Coast had significant differences. One approach was not necessarily better than the other, but they required a different set of expectations and coping skills on the part of the incoming students. In the Montana school there was zero tolerance for bullying, racial slurs, or negative comments about another person's physical appearance, sexuality, or political or religious beliefs. All of the students and the staff held each other to a high level of accountability in keeping these standards of respect. At the East Coast school, the staff encouraged the students to address these issues one-on-one if at all possible, bringing the conflicts to group counseling sessions for resolution only if the students hadn't been able to solve the problem on their own. The rationale with this approach was that the students, once they returned home, would have to deal with intolerance or bullying "in the real world," and the environment of the treatment facility gave the kids a chance to practice standing up for themselves and deflecting inappropriate remarks while still having the safety net of staff intervention if the situation got out of hand.

Naturally, you'll want to know about your child's typical daily schedule. How much time during the day will be spent in class, and how much time will be devoted to therapeutic work? How much time is dedicated to individual therapy versus group therapy? This is also a good time to clarify whether individual counseling is included in the overall cost of the program or if it will be billed separately. (We'll look more at costs in chapter 11.)

You'll also need information about family therapy—how often you'll be working with your child (most commonly over the phone, except when you do on-campus visits or family workshops where you'll meet face-to-face with your child's primary counselor and other members of the treatment team as needed) and how the time will be divided if the biological parents are divorced.

It's also a good idea to ask how group therapy sessions are going to be structured. Andy had participated in group therapy sessions before he enrolled in his emotional-growth school, but he was surprised at how long the school group sessions lasted and how intense some of those sessions became. One of the other students literally screamed in the first school group therapy session Andy attended. Had Andy known what to expect, he would not have been nearly as disconcerted.

It's important to clarify how you'll communicate with your child, the teachers, and the staff about your child's educational progress. How long will you get to talk to your child on the phone every week, and how often can you exchange letters or e-mails if the program allows it? Who, other than the parents, may your child call and write? Siblings and grandparents are usually on the approved list depending on the family situation, but communication with peers at home is often restricted until the end of the treatment program or is not allowed at all.

Which staff members are with the students in their dorms at night and on weekends? What oversight is given to make sure that the actions of the staff members are appropriate—how do they strike that tough balance between supervising your child and also respecting physical boundaries and giving your child some privacy? And finally, where do the staff and counselors go for their own therapy? Working with troubled adolescents for extended periods of time is not easy, as you well know. Even the healthiest and strongest individuals can wear down in these intense environments. How does the school take care of their own, and how do they address significant conflict between students and one of the professionals entrusted with caring for them?

This is a tremendous amount of information to process, especially when you're under the strain of moving your child. Airline pilots have checklists, surgical teams in operating rooms count instruments before and after procedures, and parents going through the turmoil you're experiencing deserve a checklist of their own. On page 63 you'll find a list of the most essential questions you'll need to ask before you make a final placement decision for your teenager. And lest all these questions seem too overwhelming to ask in a one-day school tour, remember that your educational consultant can provide much of this information. You can also access much of what you'll need from the parent handbooks or the school's website.

Consider reading chapter 3 of Reamer and Siegel's book, *Teens in Crisis*, as you make your final decision about placing your son or daughter in a residential therapeutic program. Their research should not turn you away from therapeutic schools as a whole, but it will give you a sobering look at what can happen when students are not properly supervised and when sound educational and therapeutic practices are not employed. And more efficient oversight in the industry is certainly warranted. As Reamer and Siegel write, "No single entity—private or governmental—has overarching authority to monitor, investigate, and prosecute negligent and abusive programs and schools in the struggling teens industry. Oversight is fragmented and piecemeal. Different regulatory functions are performed by different oversight agencies."[50]

Beginning in 2003, the therapeutic boarding school industry came under increasing scrutiny after a *New York Times* exposé of the physical and psychological abuse of students at a WWASPS (World Wide Association of Specialty Programs and Schools) facility in Costa Rica. WWASPS was an umbrella organization of interconnected companies that provided residential services to struggling teens and their families. WWASPS facilities are no longer in operation, but they continue to operate on a more limited basis through their website, which refers users to seven "enrollment services." These services go by the names of: Teens in Crisis, Teens Solutions [*sic*], Teen Help, Cross Creek Administration, Help My Teen, Lifelines Family Resources, and Parent Resources Hotline.[51]

Parents are advised to avoid WWASPS spin-off programs as well as programs which go by the names of SEED, Straight Inc., SAFE, and North Star Expeditions. These programs do not employ educational or therapeutic best practices which are backed up by valid, reliable research, and your child may not be well served or safe in these environments.

Three years after the *New York Times* exposé, journalist and television producer Maia Szalavitz published *Help at Any Cost: How the Troubled-Teen Industry Cons Parents and Hurts Kids*, which further examined the abuse and negligence occurring at a handful of emotional-growth schools across the country. The public outcry after the release of the book led to the first statewide attempts to examine quality control in the industry and prevent abuses, and Szalavitz's work served as the springboard for the establishment of ASTART (Alliance for the Safe, Therapeutic & Appropriate Use of Residential Treatment), which operates under the auspices of the University of South Florida and the Bazelon Center for Mental Health Law.

Alarmed by the information he received about the WWASPS controversy and Szalavitz's investigative work, US Representative George Miller of California introduced a bill to Congress seeking federal legislation for more oversight and regulation of therapeutic schools and residential treatment facilities. The bill, known as the End Institutionalized Abuse Against Children Act of 2005, was defeated, but the debate is far from over, and Utah's legislature did recently pass a similar bill into state law. Until there are federal guidelines and adequate enforcement of best practices in the therapeutic boarding school industry, "parents must look to a patchwork of academic and healthcare licenses and accreditations to judge quality."[52]

Do your research, get strong references for the program you are considering from your educational consultant and hopefully other professionals and families who have experience with the clinical staff and approaches, but most importantly, trust your own gut reaction. If you walk away from a school tour or information session with a negative feeling, take a second look if possible or consider other options. Conversely, understand that there is no ideal school—every facility is going to have its strengths and weaknesses.

chapter 11

Paying for It: Insurance and Financing the Costs of Therapeutic Schools

We didn't want to make Andy or Sarah feel guilty about the costs of their therapeutic programs—additional guilt and shame were the last things they needed as they worked through their problems—but we did want them to understand how significant the costs were, and how it was going to impact where they could go to college and how much they would need to work once they got there (if they got there).

To put things in perspective, it cost less for my daughter's four-year undergraduate program at the University of Chicago than for just under two years of residential therapeutic treatment for Andy. Our oldest daughter's PhD was a bargain compared to the nearly $7,000 a month we were spending for Sarah's emotional-growth school in North Carolina. I grimly realized we could have put Andy in a four-star hotel with a private tutor for what a dorm room in a Salt Lake City suburb was costing us. These are the sorts of expenses that ruin families financially. Yet, what else can you do? These are our children; their health, their educations, even their lives are on the line. —R. H.

THE COST OF therapeutic schools is astronomical. To tell you anything other than that would be to mislead you and make your financial planning for these programs more difficult. The average cost of an emotional-growth or therapeutic boarding school in 2005 was between $30,000 and $50,000 per academic year.[53] In our estimation, those numbers are on the low side.

Obviously the annual costs have risen significantly since Hechinger and Chaker's 2005 survey. Anecdotally, from Elizabeth's experience, tuition can range from $5,000 per month to over $11,000 per month depending on the clinical sophistication of the program. Short-term programs such as rehab or wilderness quote a per diem charge. To attract and retain the most clinically competent staff and teachers, and to provide clean and healthy living facilities and dietary programs, therapeutic schools must charge what they do. This is not the time to shop for bargains.

This general cost estimate of $60,000 or more annually often will not include additional family therapy sessions, follow-up testing and assessment, or the travel costs for you and your child for campus workshops and home visits. Often the schools will provide optional field trips or group excursions for which you'll be billed separately, and you must also remember to figure the cost of your educational consultant's services into your total bill. The IECA has recently published the average costs for educational consulting services depending on the region of the country, and those costs can be accessed on the IECA website.

It's a challenging responsibility to find the money to take care of our children without ruining our families financially. There is no academic "merit money" for therapeutic programs; no Title IX athletic scholarships to help defer the expense. Your family health insurance will likely cover some, but certainly not all, of the direct therapeutic costs. Check your policy and speak openly with your agent about your situation. In most cases, mental health coverage will be limited to a certain number of therapy sessions for a restricted time period; it will probably not be open-ended. It is unlikely that your health insurance will cover any of the educational portion of the emotional-growth school costs. Most of the programs have financial aid available for families, but you'll want to look carefully at the costs of such aid packages compared with conventional loans. Unfortunately, any money you and your family may have already set aside in a 529 plan cannot be used for therapeutic schools or services.

In some cases, state monies may be available if your child needs services that are not provided by your local school system but are mandated by the child's IEP. Once again, access to these funds varies from state to state. Do not assume that tapping into these public funds is going to be quick or easy. It will take determination and substantial effort on your part.

Some schools do have scholarship money in place for children whose families are in financial distress, and the school administration may be willing to work with you to reduce their rates at least temporarily if you can demonstrate financial need. When the program directors at the residential treatment facility Andy attended in Utah found out that his younger sister was enrolled in another therapeutic program, they were willing to negotiate on Andy's tuition costs. It doesn't hurt to ask.

Trying to negotiate with insurance companies and state agencies for additional funds is challenging at any time, and doing the paperwork and making all the phone calls while your child and family are in turmoil can be even more grueling. But perseverance often does pay off. Keep trying: keep calling. Just as with routine medical insurance claims, if you're determined in your efforts, you can many times get at least a portion of the funds you need. There are actually companies who will negotiate for you, helping you get the documentation you need and expediting the application or appeal process. Ask your family physician and your educational consultant if they have any contacts or recommendations for such programs in your area. Working with a mediator or an attorney is another layer of initial expense, but it may save you money and headaches in the long run. Creativity, determination, and patience are going to be your greatest assets in the effort to meet the costs of your child's therapeutic program.

chapter 12

What About Christmas? Holidays and Home Visits During the Treatment Process

It poured down rain that Christmas Eve. It was miserable. We had decorated the tree and hung the lights without our children there, and it seemed surreal. I prepared a great dinner—lamb chops, I think, but neither one of us was hungry. I had slept for a couple of hours that afternoon, a sure sign of depression for me, and my husband fell asleep on the couch right after we finished eating. I didn't even try to wake him up. I grabbed my coat and umbrella and headed out the door by myself to the candlelight service at our church. I'd never felt as profoundly lonely as I did that night. I sat in the church pew alone in the dark, holding my candle. Usually these services were fun, even joyous, for me, but not this year. All I wanted to do was get through the night to Christmas Day when our other children would be coming. I walked outside the chapel and the rain stopped. The streetlights were reflected in the wet pavement of the parking lot, illuminating the black field of asphalt with a glow. I felt a strange sense of peace for the first time in weeks. Andy was going to be all right; we were all going to be all right. We had a long, complicated road ahead of us, but we were going to make it through.

—R. H.

EVEN BEFORE ANDY was enrolled, his Montana school made it clear that he wouldn't be able to come home for Christmas in the first year of his treatment. At first the rationale for keeping him at school over the holidays was confusing. Wouldn't it be better to have him at home—safe and feeling all the love and support from his family and friends?

At a parents' workshop held shortly after Andy enrolled, one of the former program directors at the school explained the reasons for keeping the students on campus for the first round of holidays. For students with substance abuse and alcohol issues, the emotionally charged environments and unrealistic expectations that many people have about the holidays quite often led to a relapse if the teenager went home for a visit too soon into treatment. Stress is higher and access to drugs and alcohol is typically easier during the holidays. For example, even if the parents and immediate family are diligent about keeping drugs and alcohol out of reach, it is hard to control visiting Aunt Harriet with her post-surgery pain medications or Cousin Sid around the corner with his ubiquitous bag of pot. The students need more time to practice their coping skills and to strengthen their boundaries before they encounter Aunt Harriet or Cousin Sid again. The program director emphasized that it was more effective to have home visits, especially the first few, at a more emotionally neutral time.

The same rationale applies not only for children dealing with substance abuse issues, but also for a whole range of emotional and behavioral issues. As much as we would all love that perfect Currier & Ives image of the idyllic holiday family, it usually doesn't work out that way. People get tired during the holidays, they feel stressed, and small cracks become huge fissures in our sense of perspective and our sense of humor. We tend to expect too much of ourselves and of others. Most psychologists would agree that during times of extended stress, people tend to fall back into less effective or even destructive behavior patterns. Our coping skills tend to deconstruct. Therefore, it's understandable that many programs want to keep their students in the structured treatment environment for an initial extended period to let the children practice and integrate their new, more positive coping skills before they're tested in the family fray.

However, not all schools mandate that students stay at the school for Christmas or other major religious holidays. Sarah was able to come home for both Thanksgiving and Christmas even though she was only a few months into her treatment program. All of the home visits, or furloughs as they are sometimes called, are highly structured, and this is especially true for the first couple of times your child comes home. You'll most likely sit down with your child and his or her counselor before the home visit and write down specific plans and goals about everything from bedtimes to household chores to the amount of TV or Internet access allowed. Cell phones may or may not be allowed depending on your wishes and the recommendations of the school. The type of music your child listens to and the type of movies they watch may also be censored. Likewise, your children may be discouraged or even forbidden from contacting old classmates and peers. Travel to and from the school will be tightly supervised, especially if a flight is involved, and the first few visits will be short—only a few days in length. Some extra time may be allowed for children whose parents are divorced, particularly if the parents live in different cities, but don't expect double time. You and your child may even sign a contract about the expectations and rules on home visits or parental on-campus visits.

The goal of all this formal planning, of course, is to establish the boundaries of more constructive interaction patterns for your child and the rest of the family. Practicing these new interactions takes plenty of deliberate effort, and you'll need an outline to keep everyone on track as well as a backup plan that everyone agrees to beforehand. A small emotional grease fire can be put out quickly if you have the fire extinguisher of planned responses ready to go before the visit starts, but without that fire-extinguisher plan, the whole kitchen can go up in smoke.

Your home visit plans and your campus visit plan will probably include an early exit provision as well. This provision says that if the visit between the parents and the child isn't going well, and there isn't a reasonable expectation that the circumstances will improve, then you as a parent will have the option to terminate the visit early and return your child to school. Sometimes your child can make the call to terminate or abbreviate the visit as well. Terminating a visit early is not a failure for either you or your child—far from it. If things are going sour, ending the interaction may be the best way to get back on track more quickly. It may give the treatment team the information they need to adjust your child's program or bring difficult issues to the forefront.

The formal, written home visit plans you'll complete may feel a bit intrusive or even silly on the surface, but all the restrictions are there for a reason. Just as it is critical for parents to present a united front in raising and disciplining their children, so too is it important for parents and siblings to support the programs and recommendations of the therapeutic schools. If you have a serious misgiving about any of the therapeutic work your child is doing, discuss it directly with the appropriate staff at the facility. Certainly you'll want to really listen to your child and give him or her an appropriate forum to express feelings, but you'll undermine the school's efforts and ultimately prolong or make your child's work more difficult if you disregard the program rules or are critical of the staff or the therapeutic methods in front of your son or daughter.

Andy often complained early in his treatment that everyone was ganging up on him. He had a point. His dad, his counselor, and his whole extended family were pulling in unison, working as hard as they could to get Andy the help he needed. If working together as a family unit toward a common goal constituted "ganging up" on Andy, then that's a pretty accurate description. Everyone earnestly acted in his best interests even when those actions made him uncomfortable or weren't what he wanted at the time. Teenagers are masters of manipulation and triangulation; don't fall for it. Don't let guilt or indecision sway you from following through on the school's guidelines and protocols.

You'll finish more successfully and more quickly if you stay on task, but no one said staying on task would be easy.

As important as it is to hold everyone in the therapeutic process to accountability, it's also important to give your son or daughter a way to save face or atone if he or she makes a serious mistake during the treatment process. Shaming is counterproductive, and the professionals working with your child will discuss how disciplinary actions or "do-overs" are best handled for your son or daughter's particular situation and therapeutic approach.

You will almost certainly have a phone call with your son or daughter on birthdays and on holidays when he or she isn't at home. No one needs to tell you how bittersweet those phone calls will be. You'll miss your child terribly, of course, and your child will want to come home more than ever. But remember that your child's treatment and health comes first. While Andy was tearful on the phone the first Christmas he was away, he said later that his Christmas in Montana had actually been one of the best holidays he had ever had. How in the world could that be? A blizzard had prevented some of the staff from getting to school on time, so the students had to rally themselves with the small number of counselors who were on campus to finish decorating the tree, cut extra firewood, bring the Yule log into the huge stone fireplace in the lodge, and make hot chocolate and tea for the kitchen staff and the others who were struggling in from the storm one by one. Andy was surrounded by supportive peers singing Christmas carols and drinking hot cider. They were all in the same mess that day helping each other out. They had found true community.

In planning for the holidays while your child is in treatment, flexibility is the key. Each program will have different guidelines, schedules, and expectations, and if your child regresses significantly in his or her therapeutic work, it's not unusual for them to lose a holiday furlough or home visit privilege. It's not a punishment, but rather a way to hold your son or daughter accountable and to keep them on track to meet their treatment goals. As sad as it is not to have your child home for the holidays, and as frustrating and expensive as it can be to change travel plans at the last minute, it's important to remember that the skills your child is learning and internalizing while they're away will hopefully make for much better holiday experiences for your entire family in the future.

chapter 13

Plan B: Finding Alternatives When the First Program Is Inappropriate or Ineffective for Your Child

My husband called me from some lonely stretch of highway in Idaho. It was mid-January, and he was traveling in a blinding snowstorm. Andy had been expelled from his program in Montana, and a transport team had taken him from school to a safe house near Sandpoint, Idaho. Andy was certain that his dad had come thousands of miles to take him home. But Andy wasn't coming home, not yet. His behaviors in Montana showed us how deeply troubled he was and how deeply ingrained his distorted thinking had become. When he found out he wasn't going to be rescued, Andy turned his face to the wall and wouldn't speak to his dad. Now it was up to my husband in this miserable situation and in this miserable storm to drive hundreds of miles looking for another school that could help us with a more in-depth assessment of what was going on with Andy and what help he needed. Our educational consultant gave us the names of several programs, but my husband had to actually see the facilities before he made the decision to send Andy anywhere. —R. H.

YOU DID YOUR homework. You worked with an educational consultant, you visited the schools, and you studied the research. You made the best placement decision you possibly could for your child given the information and resources you had at the time, but the program isn't working. Now what?

You know already that different schools and residential treatment facilities will deal with specific problems at specific levels of severity. Valid, reliable assessment of your child is critical on the front end of the treatment process to establish which programs and approaches are most likely to be effective, but psychologists and educators are hesitant, and for good reason, to hang a diagnosis or a label on a child prematurely. In many cases, it's tough for even experienced psychologists or psychiatrists to identify certain disorders when the adolescent personality and sense of self is still under construction. What is the line, then, that separates an essentially normal child who has gotten off track with destructive patterns of behavior from the child who is at risk for true mental illness?

Most clinicians examine three critical areas in looking for this answer: persistence of symptoms, severity of symptoms (especially in regard to how they are impacting the child's and the family's day-to-day functioning), and resistance to conventional therapeutic approaches. As we discussed earlier, nearly every emotional-growth school will have a set of goals or steps your child will be expected to achieve in his or her academic and therapeutic work. If months go by and your child is not making progress toward meeting those goals, you'll need to work with the clinicians and teachers at the facility to do further assessment that will help you determine if your child is in the right place or not. A word of caution is merited here: It's not unusual for a teenager to make significant educational or emotional gains in a therapeutic school and then go through a period of regression. While the step back can be frustrating for you and your child, it doesn't mean that overall progress isn't being made. That's why it's so important to quantify and identify those goals when possible, so on the dark days when you feel the protocol isn't working, you and your child can look back objectively and see how far you've come.

The village approach of the whole treatment team working to observe and help your child should quickly validate the original school recommendations and placement, or conversely, you should know within a few months if there are problems and issues that weren't uncovered in the original diagnostic work. One mother we interviewed commented that the initial focus on her son's educational work dealt with his ADD/ADHD, but it wasn't until Gary was in a small class-room at his therapeutic school with plenty of one-on-one attention that teachers realized Gary's primary learning problem was dyslexia. Once the staff identified and addressed the dyslexia, managing the ADD and Gary's frustration and emotional issues became much easier.

If you find that your child's school isn't the right placement, your educational consultant or the facility's staff can make recommenda-tions and referrals for you to schedule additional testing. The school may be able to do some of the testing in-house or make arrangements with their adjunct staff or outside contractors to complete more assess-ments. Naturally, parents always have the option of using an outside testing facility if they have any concerns about the objectivity of the in-house test results. Usually all the testing can be done on a day-student schedule, but if your child needs to stay overnight for more extensive testing or observation, there are facilities designed for that type of work in most urban areas.

You'll remember from our discussion of the different types of schools that therapeutic work becomes progressively more intense from emotional-growth schools to therapeutic schools to residential treatment centers. In residential treatment centers, the students have usually been diagnosed with a mental health disorder. Their behaviors are more likely to be a threat to their own safety or to the safety of others than the behaviors of their counterparts in emotional-growth or therapeutic schools.[54]

Most therapeutic schools and RTCs will have a list of negative behaviors that are grounds for the student's immediate dismissal from the program. That list will be clearly communicated to your child and your family from the very beginning of the treatment process. These rules are in place to protect the other children and the staff, and to limit the facility's liability. The rules differ somewhat from school to school, but the typical grounds for immediate dismissal are:

- Running away from school
- Using drugs or alcohol on campus (other than the prescribed medications in the proper dosage)
- Using violence or the threat of violence toward other students or staff
- Acting out sexually with another student
- Setting fires or other deliberately destructive acts

The school may give your child a second chance or a reprieve based on the situation, but you can't count on it. And if the behavior occurs again, it's almost certain your child will be expelled. If you can't pick up your child immediately, the school may have your child stay in a different part of the facility with heavy staff supervision until you can take your son or daughter home or to another facility. Depending on the severity of the situation, the program directors may make arrangements for your child to be escorted off campus to a safe house immediately by a transport service (much like the ones used to take students to wilderness programs). From personal experience, the situations are frightening, exhausting, and expensive. The chances of your child being dismissed from a therapeutic program are small, but if these circumstances do arise, you'll need to know what you are facing and be willing to act quickly to find another placement. Once again, an experienced educational consultant is indispensable at a time such as this.

If after two or three placements your child is still struggling and not making progress toward his or her therapeutic goals, you may be faced with another round of diagnostic work. At this point, a short-term psychiatric hospital program may be your best option, and while it is beyond the scope of this book to identify those facilities, your psychiatrist or psychologist will have referral information for you. Don't despair if your child needs this level of help—specialized help for teenagers and young adults is available from competent, compassionate therapists and physicians in several excellent facilities across the country.

Hopefully your child's first placement will be the right one, and the facility can provide the educational and therapeutic environment best suited to your family's needs. It's important to be realistic and acknowledge that your child's issues may change during the course of treatment or that additional diagnostic work or observation may make it necessary for you to alter treatment plans or locations. If you have to change schools, you can, and your educational consultant and the school administrators will help you make the necessary transitions.

chapter 14

Considerations for Adopted Children

Crouching uncomfortably on a log in the cold winter morning, I listened intently as the therapist pulled Erica back into the memories of her childhood, back to the seemingly unreachable depths of infancy. I was trying to hold back my tears, half wondering if they would freeze in the single-digit temperatures, but mostly afraid that my gestures to wipe them away would interrupt the powerful session of remembrance. Here we were, miles from base camp, side by side by side, facing a fire pit with no fire, and nothing but white as far as my eyes could see. Erica's world, though, was colored by emotion—both anger and sadness. In a deeply relaxed, almost hypnotic state, Erica breathed slowly and rhythmically as she expressed her deepest feelings of inadequacy and rejection. I didn't need to know Erica's story to understand her grief, but it was obvious that she had begun the process of reconciliation.

Like most of the girls at this wilderness program, Erica had been adopted as a baby. Now she was a teenage girl trying to make sense of her loss, trying to understand who she was and why she wasn't good enough for her birth parents to keep her. She was in a group of girls who had reason to feel abandoned by people who should have loved them. Erica was making good progress, and it was because of her relative self-awareness that I was allowed to observe. Using an innovative therapeutic technique called brainspotting, the therapist focused Erica's conscious thoughts on past traumas in order to extinguish the memories of those traumas. Slowly, the therapist brought the session to a close with soothing words of encouragement and validation for good work. Exhausted, yet at the same time energized and ravenous from the experience (me too), Erica scampered back up the hill to rejoin her group. Erica's therapist and I stood for a brief moment in conversation. I wanted to know so much more, to understand on a deeper level. But, as my time in the woods of northern Wisconsin had come to an end, I hoisted my pack, turned, and followed a different path. —E. D.

Every parent reading this book has his or her own particular set of circumstances that has led them down the path of seeking residential therapeutic treatment for their child. Obviously, it would be impossible to address each unique situation or provide comprehensive recommendations on the best protocol for individual families or issues. However, the topic of adoption merits special consideration. The problems that face adopted children and their families present themselves time and time again in Elizabeth's practice. At any one time, adopted children comprise between 60 and 80 percent of her caseload. Anecdotally, many residential programs and schools report that adopted children make up more than half of their student populations. *The overarching question is: Why do adopted children and adolescents seem to have more cognitive, emotional, and behavioral issues than children who are raised with their biological parents?* Parents and families of adopted children face this critical question every day, and there is no simple answer. From drug and alcohol abuse in utero, trauma from the loss of a parent, to abuse and neglect while in foster care or orphanages, there are myriad factors that drive adoptive parents to seek therapeutic care for their children.

According to Dr. Margaret Keyes of the Minnesota Center for

Twin and Family Research, it has long been speculated that adopted children are "over-represented in mental health settings."[55] Dr. Keyes found in her study of infant adoptions that DSM-IV disorders are more commonly seen in adopted children than non-adopted children. More specifically, she found that adopted children are twice as likely to have disorders such as ADHD, oppositional defiant disorder (ODD), conduct disorder, major depressive disorder (MDD), and separation anxiety disorder (SAD) as non-adopted children.[56] With only 2 percent of our nation's children adopted, those statistics are staggering.[57] Although Dr. Keyes' research is just one source addressing the complexities of adoption, her work has added a depth and breadth of knowledge to our society as a whole.

To gain some insight into the challenges that affect adopted children, we need to do a brief overview of the current research on adoption, especially as it relates to attachment theory. Psychologist John Bowlby first described modern attachment theory in the early 1950s. Bowlby asserted that the bonding experience that takes place between a parent and child is based primarily on security, proximity, and safety. He went on to say that children become emotionally attached to their early caregivers regardless of the quality of care they receive. Furthermore, children begin to develop a working model of expectations and of how their needs are going to be met. Healthy attachments are based on a reciprocal relationship between parents/caregivers and the child. As human beings we have a biological need to connect; we need to know that in times of distress, someone who loves and cares for us will be available for comfort. From birth, we have a need to make sense of things, to begin the narrative that will determine how future relationships will develop. From the very beginning, we get the meaning of the world from our parents.

In later research, Mark T. Greenberg outlined four goals in examining attachment theory.[58] The first goal is to "provide a critical developmental framework for understanding how early and continued close relationships affect the cognitive-affective structures that children use to construct their expectancies, views of the world, and coping strategies." Next, examining the theory helps us understand more clearly the psychopathology that can develop in children when there is an "absence of a significant attachment relationship, significant distortions in the quality of care, or traumatic disruptions or losses of attachment in childhood." Third, understanding the implications of attachment theory helps clinicians understand the adult behavior of adoptees in light of how their thoughts, emotions, and expectations about affection and relationships are influenced by those early caregiving experiences. And finally, understanding attachment theory helps clinicians provide improved services to children in the areas of parental caretaking, adoption, foster care, and even institutional care. By informing practitioners, foster and adoptive parents, and policymakers on the implications of attachment theory, we'll hopefully have a clearer path in the future to providing preventive strategies or early intervention to adopting families.

Adopted children endure a special set of emotional issues that tend to reemerge during adolescence:

- Identity
- Rejection and Abandonment
- Grief/Loss
- Guilt and Shame

As they enter adolescence, adopted children are likely to present the following questions:

1. Who are my real parents?
2. Who am I? Who do I identify with—my birth family or my adoptive family?
3. Which cultural or religious heritage do I claim?
4. Why did my birth mother give me away? What did I do wrong?
5. Why did she keep my siblings but give me away?
6. Why do I have to be adopted?

Another interesting factor to consider in the high number of adopted children who are candidates for therapeutic schools is the adoptive parents themselves—but not in the way one might initially think. Are adoptive parents better educated than the general public? Do they recognize more quickly when their adopted child needs help, and are they more willing than biological parents to seek out that help? Because of the counseling and information parents receive as they go through the adoption process, are they better able to access the resources and help that their children need? Much more research is needed.

chapter 15

Holding Fast: Keeping Yourself and Your Relationships Healthy

While Your Child Is Away

After months of family therapy sessions with Andy, dozens of on-campus workshops, and biweekly parent-teacher-counselor conference calls, my husband and I were emotionally exhausted. And at the same time, we knew Andy's and Sarah's struggles were taking a significant toll on our relationship. When someone suggested we seek marriage counseling, my tired, beleaguered husband groaned, "More therapy? More? We're in counseling sessions nearly every day. I don't think I can take any more. I feel I've been 'therapized' to death!" Ironically, Andy was saying the same thing about his own intense therapy schedule.

The wise psychologist I had been seeing on an individual basis recommended that we take a short hiatus. "What you all need is not more therapy—you and your husband need a long weekend together at the beach without your cell phones." She was right. We learned that self-care and care for our marriage were every bit as important as the care we were providing for Andy and Sarah. We took that long weekend at the beach and came back refreshed and better able to handle the pressures and challenges of the children's treatment. —R. H.

THE TIME, ENERGY, and financial resources it takes to care for your child in a residential therapeutic environment can be exhausting, and it's easy to forget to care for yourself and the other critical relationships in your life at the same time. Yet you must. It's exponentially harder to help your child at school and in the transition home if you aren't healthy and strong yourself.

In our interviews with counselors, therapists, and the other families who have gone through this ordeal, the following strategies seem to provide a reasonable method for finding balance and some sense of peace in a time with our children that is by definition unbalanced and anything but peaceful. Some of these recommendations are obvious; others are new, fresh ideas that will hopefully give you energy and respite.

a. *Use the time your child is away to do your own therapeutic work.* By the time your child has entered a wilderness program or a therapeutic school, your family will most likely have been under intense stress for months or even years. Having your child out of the house will give you the first break you may have had in a long time. Forgive yourself immediately for the sense of relief you feel. Now is your chance to exhale and take stock of the other crucial relationships in your life—your spouse or partner, your other children, your close friends. Now is the time to rest emotionally if you can and then set about the task of mending yourself and mending the fabric in other relationships that have been worn thin by your struggling child's intense need for your time and attention.

You also know by now that the therapeutic work your child is doing will involve your whole family. Transformation in attitude and behavior will mean a significant change in your family dynamics, not just in your teenager's actions. To initiate and sustain this positive change will take hard work, time, and the collaborative effort of everyone in your family, but be encouraged that this family system of therapy brings some of the best results.

b. *If you feel you've been "therapized" to death in family or individual sessions, take a short break.* Engaging in the hard work and concentration required for therapy is easier and more effective if you have a counseling time-out occasionally. It's like running a marathon but stopping every few miles to drink some water, walk, and catch your breath.

c. *Exercise, eat a healthy diet, and maintain a regular sleep schedule.* Easier said than done, isn't it? As working adults with families and other responsibilities, maintaining our own health in ordinary circumstances can be difficult. Stack up the demands of a struggling teenager against the daily routine, and working out and getting enough sleep (if you can sleep at all through the worry) become even more of a challenge. Don't beat yourself up if you can't maintain this lifestyle on a daily basis, but do make it your daily aim through small, reasonable goals. A long walk a few times a week and a night at home cooking something healthy with your spouse or a buddy will improve your emotional and your physical health.

d. *Reconnect with your other children.* In the Pulitzer Prize–winning musical *Next to Normal*, the young heroine of the play, Natalie, sings a heartbreaking song titled "Superboy and the Invisible Girl." In the lyrics Natalie expresses her anger and sadness because of her parents' unresolved grief over her older brother. No matter what Natalie does, no matter how outstanding she is as a student or a musician, her parents, especially her mother, simply do not recognize or appreciate her. They don't seem to care much about her at all; her dead brother still consumes all of her mother's love and attention. Natalie truly is the Invisible Girl.

No doubt the siblings of struggling teenagers often feel much like Natalie does. Older children may realize intellectually that they are just as loved, just as important, just as "visible" as their struggling sister or brother, but on an emotional level it's not easy for them to constantly put their needs in second place behind those of the struggling adolescent. Adult children may even withdraw or distance themselves from the family for a time because of the stress and demands of the situation. Andy's older sisters and stepsisters fully recognized that his issues were significant and that his family's efforts on his behalf were valid, but they sometimes asked for the "30,000-foot view" of Andy's problems, not every detail. It wouldn't be fair to have asked them to get fully caught up in the drama and in the vortex of Andy's struggles. They had their own families, educations, and problems to work through. They fully supported Andy, but they also asked us to maintain certain boundaries so that they could keep their own lives on a healthy track.

e. *Get away with your spouse, even if it's only for a picnic in the park or a night out at a comedy club.* The financial burden of having your child in a therapeutic boarding school may make a full vacation impossible, but be creative. Vacation in your own city; take a day to go hiking or out for a picnic. Go see a goofy comedy movie. Once again, don't repress or ignore the reality of what's going on with your teenager when you talk, but agree to talk about other things during your time away even if you have to force yourself to bring other subjects into the conversation.

f. *Practice your faith. Plug into the empowerment of meditation and prayer.*

Current research in neuroscience is revealing what people of faith have known intuitively for centuries: meditation and prayer are enormously effective tools in stress management, and the electrical activity of the brain changes significantly when prayer and/or meditation are practiced regularly.[59] We've become even more attuned to how vital prayer and meditation can be, especially when families are undergoing extended periods of stress.

Part of Andy's therapeutic regime at this point is dialectical behavioral therapy (DBT), which is deeply rooted in the principles of mindfulness, meditation, and compassion. Those principles, of course, are some of the basic tenets of Buddhism. You don't have to embrace Buddhism as your faith (or any other faith, for that matter) to fully embrace the philosophy of peacefulness and mindfulness. The more we read about different effective therapeutic practices, the more of those attributes we see put into play.

No matter what your religious beliefs may be, practicing your faith and involving the rest of your family in that practice, if they are open to it, will provide you with an excellent platform of comfort and balance. You certainly won't feel that comfort and balance all the time, but tapping into the strength of your faith will keep you from despair and help lighten the dark episodes.

g. *Practice "sour hour" venting sessions with your spouse and/or your friends, but then move on.* Everyone needs to vent about the hardships and frustrations of having a child in a therapeutic school. No matter how you look at it, the situation is tough and unsettling. You need a safe place and a trusted person with whom you can vent, rage, and bitch—whether it's about your child, the therapists, the costs, or simply the circumstances in general. Set an alarm clock or a kitchen timer with your spouse or close friend, and rant away—but when the timer goes off, you must stop your rant. Let the other person have his or her turn, or better yet, move on to another topic altogether.

You should be able to express your frustrations and sorrow, but you don't want to marinate in your problems, and you want to be careful not to let those problems increasingly define who you are as a person or who you and your spouse are as a couple. As empathetic as people want to be, until you've lived the therapeutic boarding school experience, you can't fully understand the hardships. But you'll be surprised that some of your dearest friends may end up being people who have had similar problems with their teenagers and young adult children. We understand each other; we get it; and when we get together socially, we always ask, earnestly ask, about each other's children—but we've learned not to make it the exclusive topic of conversation.

h. *Recognize and accept the fact that you're going to have bad days. Acknowledge them and start fresh the following day.* No matter how solid your ego strength, how healthy your marriage, or how well adjusted your other children may be, dealing with a struggling adolescent is going to take a heavy toll on your relationships and your pocketbook. Be as gentle with yourself, your partner, and your other family members as you can, and admit that some days are going to be just plain awful. You'll have days when you yell at your kids, say hurtful or blaming things to your spouse, or invalidate your struggling child. You are human; you are struggling too. Apologize when you have a kick-the-dog episode, and then move on. Grant yourself the same grace and latitude you strive to give others. As Emerson said: "Finish . . . every day, and be done with it. For manners, and for wise living, it is a vice to remember. You have done what you could—some blunders and absurdities no doubt crept in forget them as fast as you can tomorrow is a new day. You shall begin it well and serenely, and with too high a spirit to be cumbered with your old nonsense. This day . . . is too dear with its hopes and invitations to waste a moment on the rotten yesterdays."

i. *Do something kind for your spouse every day, and write down something you're grateful for every day as well.* What you do or say to affirm your partner doesn't have to be elaborate—it only has to be sincere. Bring your wife a cup of hot tea while she's getting ready for work in the morning; pour your husband a glass of wine as you sit down together at the end of the day. Cue his favorite song on the car stereo; tell her how much you appreciate her hard work or a home-cooked meal. Be kind to each other. You're going to need each other. You will need to pull together to help your marriage and your child survive and flourish again. It may sound a bit contrived to keep a gratitude list, but writing things down gives you a small daily discipline which makes you realize how much you have to be thankful for even in the midst of the hardship with your children. It helps you keep a sense of perspective.

The intensive residential therapy process with an adolescent is a long trek, but hopefully as you employ the strategies we've suggested, your other relationships will be healthier, and you'll manage to carve out some time to take care of yourself as well. You can expect to be emotionally weary throughout much of your child's treatment, but you shouldn't have to face every day feeling exhausted.

chapter 16

Homecoming: Discharge Plans and Preparing for Your Child's Transition Back

My husband and I listened with delight and some amusement to Andy counsel a friend of his in New York over the phone one night. He urged her not to go out with certain people or to certain places in the city. "You're going to put yourself under too much pressure," he said. "You're going to have too much temptation in your path. I want you healthy and happy. Stay away from those people and those places that got you into trouble before."

Was this really Andy talking? All of a sudden he was a gentle and empathetic friend with much more insight than a typical seventeen-year-old boy. It was a glimpse of the good man and the good parent he'll hopefully be one day. —R. H.

AS YOUR CHILD and your family progress through the therapeutic work the school provides, your son or daughter's home visits and off-campus visits will become longer and more frequent. You will still have structure and boundaries for those visits, but your child will be given more freedom and privileges. One of the mothers we interviewed was particularly insightful about the homecoming preparations. "You realize," she said, "that the therapeutic school wasn't a fix or a cure. It's a springboard for your kid. It's a place where they can learn and practice the coping skills they're going to need when they get home. You also realize that you have to strike some sort of balance. You can't do everything for your child, but you can't completely abdicate the discipline and structure your child needs to a school or a therapist either."

Families can't gloss over or minimize the importance of the discharge plan, the formal, written recommendations from the treatment team about your child's follow-up care when he or she returns home. At least a couple of months before the end of the program, you and your child will begin meeting with your child's therapists and teachers to begin putting together the plan for your child's transition home. Everyone is excited, everyone is upbeat, and everyone gets to contribute his or her two cents into the plan. But as the sign says in the cafeteria of Acadia Village (now called Village Behavioral Health), a residential treatment center outside Knoxville, Tennessee, "Don't forget in the dark what you learned in the light." Temper your excitement with realistic expectations. It's natural to be both excited and anxious about your child's return.

Your discharge plan may recommend that your child attend a traditional day or boarding school, an alternative high school, or even a step-down program with therapeutic elements in the academic setting to help your child with the transition back. There will also be recommendations about how frequently your son or daughter should see a counselor after returning home, and often suggestions about which therapeutic approaches are likely to be most successful. You'll once again find invaluable support from your educational consultant, who can help you with the logistics of getting your child ready and registered for these different programs.

Just as with home furloughs and off-campus visits, your discharge plan will include specific boundaries you'll negotiate with your child about computer usage, driving privileges, contact with former friends, academic expectations . . . the list of house rules may be extensive. It's critical to have these rules in place and secure buy-in from your child and the other family members to make the transition smoother. Everyone needs to be on the same page about expectations, and it will take commitment and discipline to hold the discharge plan and house rules in place once your child gets home. The plan should also include follow-up conference calls and therapy sessions with the staff of the therapeutic school in the early weeks of transition.

As your child returns to routine life, he will naturally question and challenge the house rules, especially if he is performing well at school and handling the emotional demands of his new schedule. Stay focused. The more structure and routine your family can maintain in the first year your child is back, the better. Educational consultants and program directors agree that the best long-term results occur when the discharge plan is followed closely.

However, you have to be flexible. No one can hold to a discharge plan perfectly, and the events and circumstances your family encounters in the transition will make some adjustments necessary. Andy got his cell phone back much earlier than intended because he made a compelling case about needing to reach his parents for practical matters and also to let them know if he had periods of serious anxiety or depression while he was at school. He also wanted desperately to be a "regular kid" again, and having the use of a cell phone (albeit severely limited at first) gave him a much-needed sense of normalcy among his peers.

As with all transitions, it's two steps forward, one step back. You'll have difficult days with your child, days when you wonder if the program did any good at all. You'll also have days when you're delighted with your child and the progress she's made. It's expected that after a short honeymoon phase of homecoming, your child will have at least one period of significant regression. While frustrating, these episodes of regression are part of the overall return to balance. Do all you can to remember that on the rough reentry days.

Sarah's emotional-growth school played basketball, soccer, and volleyball with several of the traditional boarding schools and day schools nearby, and nearly every weekend the girls had an opportunity to earn off-campus passes to shop, go to craft or arts fairs, and participate in the dozens of outdoor activities available in the mountains near Asheville, North Carolina. All that contact with the broader community and the girls from other schools made Sarah's early transition home much easier on several levels than her brother's. By definition, the more restricted environment of the RTC kept Andy out of mainstream culture for nearly two years, and diving back into social situations and even going to the mall often felt strange and unsettling for him. He said once that he felt a little bit like a soldier coming back from a foreign country into a flood of material and sensory input.

Your child has learned a whole new vocabulary and set of coping skills through his therapeutic work, and when he employs those skills, he'll often outpace his peers in decision-making and relationships. He may also remain strong friends with some of the other adolescents he met in treatment. The solidarity and support Andy gets from his peers at the Montana school are helping him and enriching his life even several years after his return home. He has friends all over the country, and they make a huge effort to stay in touch.

The formal discharge plan and the follow-up counseling you'll receive from your child's program will give you a strong framework on which to build your child's transition back, but remember, it's a plan, not a script. There is no way to anticipate some of the problems and challenges your family will encounter when your child comes home. Stick to the discharge plan as closely as you reasonably can and accept that after the "honeymoon phase" of the first few days and weeks, your child may have a period of regression. The program hasn't failed and you haven't failed. Instead, this is the real-life opportunity to test and reinforce the skills and coping mechanisms both you and your child have been practicing throughout their treatment.

CONCLUSION

A PARENT'S EXPERIENCE

Did it work? Was it worth it? Was the year Sarah spent away and the nearly two years that Andy spent in therapeutic schools and residential treatment facilities worth the heartache and the cost? For our family, the answer is a happy but qualified yes. And the answer is still evolving.

Andy has significant mental health issues that can't be quickly "fixed" or "cured." His illness has to be managed like any other chronic health problem. We'd be using the same holistic approach of healthy lifestyle, professional support, and appropriate medications if Andy had asthma or diabetes. And with each passing day, we have to allow Andy to become more self-sufficient in managing his illness.

A few months ago, I picked Andy and one of his friends up from school and listened to them laugh and talk constantly on the twenty-minute ride home. Later that afternoon Andy bounded out the door grinning about his two-hour driving lesson on the notorious Atlanta expressways. He was about as happy and upbeat as a teenager could possibly be. Less than forty-eight hours later, he was so depressed he could hardly muster the energy to go with his father for a haircut. We couldn't see any environmental triggers that caused the dive. We can't explain it, and we can't control it, but at least now we have a set of skills for Andy to use, a set of firebreaks if you will, that keep his moods from escalating out of control.

Andy had the expected honeymoon phase once he returned home from school, followed by a serious regression. We needed to hospitalize Andy for several weeks. After his return from the hospital, however, he made steady progress. Once his mood stabilized and he felt stronger, I asked Andy if he thought he might have been better off, or as well off, if he had gone straight to the hospital instead of going through all the months away at school. His answer was quick and unequivocal. "I learned a lot at Silver Hill [the psychiatric hospital in Connecticut where he was a patient], and I learned it fast, but I don't think I would have been ready for it if I hadn't been through all the treatment I went through at school. All the skills built on each other."

My husband and I have to be on constant guard not to let our moods get tied up with Andy's. When Andy first returned home, we'd be ebullient on the days he was up and functioning well, but low and extremely discouraged on the days when he struggled. We're learning, slowly, to disengage our own feelings from Andy's, and to disengage our love for this amazing, endearing young man from our fear of his disorder. It's not a quick or easy process, and we're thankful for the excellent team of therapists and physicians who care for Andy and support our work. We're also extremely thankful for each other and for the relative balance and calm of our older children.

As I write this, Andy has been accepted to the School of the Art Institute of Chicago, one of the leading art schools in the country, based on the strength of his photography portfolio. When Andy's acceptance letter came along with a substantial merit scholarship offer, I cried. Andy cried. His dad teared up. The merit money wasn't nearly what our costs had been for Andy's treatment, but it made a big dent in what had been exorbitant tuition and fees.

Andy is deservedly proud of what he has done in treatment and the merit scholarship he earned. His experience in treatment inspires and informs his work as a photographer. He's not "paying it back";

he's "paying it forward" in the creativity and insight of his art. A family couldn't ask for any more. The boy we feared might never finish high school is packing his bags for Chicago and is now on his college journey and making his way in the world. His therapeutic school experience truly was the springboard. Two years in a supportive academic environment with like-minded peers helped him finish the work. The work of phenomenal counselors, physicians, and nearly two years of intensive dialectical behavioral therapy helped finish the work. The affirmation of his family helped finish the work, but of course, we all know that the work is never really finished—for Andy or for any of us. We're all on a lifelong path of healing and reconciliation.

Sarah's therapeutic work was sidetracked when the emotional-growth school she attended in North Carolina was closed. Nothing ominous happened with the program or Sarah; the organization that operated the school simply decided to switch its focus from general therapeutic work to a specialty program to help adolescents who were dealing with Asperger's syndrome. Sarah came home from the program several months before her work was finished and adequately internalized. Sarah flourished at her new school and with her new peer group for a few months after she got back to Atlanta, but soon old problems and patterns reemerged. After one school year, Sarah wanted to move to the smaller alternative high school that her brother attended. She wanted a more supportive academic and emotional environment. As always, her grades were outstanding, even though her constant need to challenge her teachers and her coaches made us cringe from time to time.

Unfortunately, after another school term, Sarah was struggling emotionally again, and the issues she faced, while different from Andy's, were every bit as serious if not more so. Recently, Sarah completed the wilderness program at Open Sky in Colorado, and she is now enrolled in a residential treatment center in Utah. Our experience with Sarah is a cautionary tale for other families; programs need time and reinforcement to "stick" and accomplish change. You can't rush or force a treatment program or follow an arbitrary schedule. Hopefully, Sarah will have a chance to complete her therapeutic work at this RTC, and we'll see the same excellent results with Sarah that we've seen with her brother. The journey continues. . . .

A PROFESSIONAL'S INSIGHT

How can parents avoid the problems that lead to the consideration of therapeutic schools in the first place? And if we can't totally avoid the problems, what can we do as parents and as a community to at least improve our children's chances of weathering the storm of adolescence more successfully? Intuitively, most parents think that spending time with their children will help, that taking an interest in their academics and extracurricular activities will help, that having reasonable boundaries regarding the Internet, cell phones, and peers will help—but does all that really make any difference? What does the research, even with flawed methodology, really tell us?

This time, parental intuition is spot-on. Researchers have looked closely at the factors that increase adolescent resilience in different arenas of behavior and performance, and it is true that parental presence and involvement are critical. Simply being there and showing up for the volleyball game or the school play goes a long way to ensuring your child's success, but obviously as a parent you're going to need to do much more. Having meals together with your children as many times a week as possible is particularly important, as is showing a genuine interest in their schoolwork and outside interests.

You can't do it alone, though. One of the most important factors in teenage resilience and success is the presence of a mentor, another strong adult to whom your adolescent can go for advice or simply to express her feelings. A coach, a teacher, a youth minister, an extended family member with whom your child has a strong connection—any and all of these people are instrumental in giving your child another line of defense in handling the stress of adolescence. Practicing your faith is another crucial area of support. Research shows that students who are actively involved in their faith community, no matter what that faith might be, are less likely to abuse alcohol or drugs, are less likely to drop out of school, and tend to become sexually active at a later age.[60]

Based on the consistent results of research, it seems reasonable to suggest a "Big Five" in helping your children through the rigors of teenage life in the twenty-first century:

1. Sit down for an evening meal together at least two or three times a week, and if your schedule won't permit gathering around the dinner table, then make plans for Saturday breakfast together or Sunday lunches. If your schedule is too busy to accommodate that, then your schedule is too busy, and you need to rethink your priorities.

2. Allow your children cell phones and social networking if you think it's appropriate, but monitor what they're doing and with whom. Have a time limit for your child to be on the Internet, Facebook, Twitter, or whatever the latest social networking hub might be, and keep your child accountable by requiring her to turn in her computer and phone for a certain time if she breaks the boundaries you've decided upon.

3. Present a united front with your spouse or ex-spouse in issues of discipline and boundaries. If you disagree strongly with your partner's approach to handling a problem with your child, discuss that disagreement in private, far out of earshot of your teenager. Teenagers (and even more critically, younger children) need to know that their parents are competent and in charge to have a solid feeling of security. Your children may complain bitterly about the structure and the rules, but they need them in order to develop their own self-discipline. Be a parent, not a buddy. Respect the input and advice of counselors, but don't abdicate parenting to them or defer important decisions to them.

4. Show your children how to fight fair. Teach them how to attack issues and problems, not other individuals in the family or community. Even if you have to stage the fight, you need to model clearly for your children that conflict, handled in the appropriate way, can actually strengthen relationships. Give your kids the skills to argue, negotiate, and resolve problems.

5. Practice your faith, acknowledging that teenagers and young adults will often push back against the belief system that their families embrace. Your child may refuse formal worship services, but give him or her other options to serve in the community. Focusing outward to the needs of others will give your adolescent a much-needed sense of perspective about the relative severity of his own problems. Building a house with Habitat for Humanity, cleaning up a local stream, or sorting food at a neighborhood food bank are all great ways for your teenager to reach out, and those activities are even more impactful when you do them as a family.

The earlier you start the Big Five with your family, the better. You're going to get more and more resistance to these activities as your children hit puberty, but if the patterns are firmly established, you can hang on to some of the traditions until the maelstrom of adolescence is over. All of these family practices help, but there is still no guarantee that our teenagers won't struggle significantly and for long periods of time despite all our best efforts. We can't control our genes and family history, and we can't keep the onslaught of negative media out of our children's lives either.

As your child approaches late adolescence and young adulthood, some elements of cognitive and emotional maturity snap into place naturally, developmentally . . . thankfully. You will realize, as will your sons or daughters, that ultimately their choices and their lives are their own. We can do our best to shepherd them through the teenage years, but we can't live their lives for them or make their decisions. In the end, they are responsible for their choices and the consequences of those choices. Our most important task as parents is to give our children the skills and resources they need to eventually stand on their own.

ACKNOWLEDGMENTS

When I think about the number of people who have worked to make the publication of this book possible, I'm astounded. I'm also humbled. Many of the individuals who contributed to this book also played a significant part in the therapeutic treatment of our children. The network stretches all across the United States and into Canada. My first thank you, however, goes to someone close to home. Nancy Binkow, a longtime friend and neighbor, introduced me to Elizabeth Donnelly when she realized that both of us had an interest in writing about therapeutic schools. Without that introduction, this book most certainly wouldn't exist.

I also owe a huge debt of gratitude to Lisa Huber, MD, whose insight and expertise as a physician kept us grounded and hopeful during Andy's therapeutic work. I am also indebted to her for referring us to Jean Hague, the exceptional educational consultant who helped us chart the course for Andy's therapeutic placements and who stuck by us throughout the entire process. Not only is Jean an outstanding educational consultant, but she is also a great lady in every sense of the word.

To Erin Dixon, Rashidah Bowen, and Dr. Billy Peebles of the Lovett School, thank you for your compassion and understanding as

Andy left Atlanta and began his treatment. I also want to extend my thanks to Dr. Martha Burdette, Dr. Wood Smethurst, Mrs. Kecia May, and the other dedicated and innovative educators at the Ben Franklin Academy in Decatur, Georgia. You all provided the optimal learning environment for Andy's transition back home. You gave him a place to flourish academically and creatively.

We've been fortunate beyond words to work with teams of committed and effective counselors, professionals who helped not only Andy and Sarah, but also our entire extended family. We couldn't have done it without the excellent clinical skills of George Ellis and Ashley Wade or without the nurture and support of Eric Yost and Charles Jones. I also want to thank the medical and clinical staff of Silver Hill Hospital in Connecticut for the amazingly effective work they accomplished with Andy while he was a patient there.

In Atlanta, I want to thank Betsy Craig, Minal Shaw, and especially Mary Stewart Peden for the guidance and validation they gave everyone in our family. To the other families at the Atlanta Dialectical Behavioral Therapy Center, thank you for working shoulder to shoulder with us each week and for teaching us that "it's not the lyric, it's the music" that matters most in communicating love and affirmation to our struggling teenagers. As much as anything, I am grateful for the insight and direction I got from Rev. Ron Greer and Dr. Kelli Bynum about the complicated diagnosis and treatment of borderline personality disorder. Thank you for the encouragement and empathy when I needed it most, and for steering me to the most clearly written research in the field.

To Bill and Nancie Carmichael and Rhonda Funk, thank you for such a gentle and ethical introduction to the publishing world. To Rachel Starr Thomson, what a gifted editor you are! Thank you again for helping us polish up the initial drafts of *Second Shelter.* I also want to thank Kathy Cromartie for her patience and diligence in typing our revisions. I'm also grateful for the support that Wendy Lee and Kara Davis, our editors at Lantern, have given us and this manuscript.

Thank you for helping us open the door to a sometimes confusing and inaccessible part of the mental health care community.

For Holly, Anna, Meg, Katie, Walt, and Adam, thank you for hiking this long trek with us and for being stalwart and patient even when we weren't. Thank you, Sam, for being the son I never had and for always paying it forward. And finally, thank you, Reg, for being the most loving and supportive spouse on the planet and the best father any child could ever hope for. —R. H.

In the fall of 2010, as I was recovering from a broken leg, a good friend decided I needed something to get my mind off the unrelenting tedium of homebound life. It was quite an effort to get me out of the house and to my favorite lunch spot, but my friend was convinced that female camaraderie was just the thing to lift my spirits. Thank you Nancy Binkow for caring and for introducing me to Rebecca Haid. Without both of these women, *Second Shelter* would still be just an idea tucked into the reaches of my mind. Rebecca, you truly are the driving force behind this book. Your patience and calm presence provided the balance to see this project through to the end. Thank you for sharing your story.

In my profession, countless hours are spent on the road evaluating schools and programs to provide my clients the most current information available. Without my travel buddies, Pam Tedeschi and Debbie Shawen, these journeys would be lonely indeed. We've had some great laughs and shared some amazing adventures, but most importantly, we've learned together. We are the three amigas!

Second Shelter would not be possible if not for my client families. I am blessed that I can be a part of your lives. I know how difficult it is to develop the trust needed to open hearts and expose wounds so that healing can begin. Above all, thank you to my students. You are worthy and have so much to offer our world—some of you just don't know it yet.

Endless gratitude goes to Dr. Paul Case, who encouraged me to reach out to Lantern Books. Your advice was invaluable. I am indebted to Wendy Lee and Kara Davis of Lantern Books who have been so open and accepting of this manuscript. I know in my heart that *Second Shelter* will resonate with families who struggle with situations beyond their control and will be a trusted resource for professionals who provide guidance to these families.

Thank you to Alison Schultz, my good friend and my priest, whose wisdom, counsel, and wicked sense of humor make life a little bit easier to bear. I like to think we help each other. Thank you to Kyle Young, who inspires me and gives me confidence, Elaine Morgan, who is the earth mother of all mothers, and Lisa Shunnarah, who helps me keep it real.

My children and my husband are my life. Clayton, you are the kindest, most gentle man on this earth. I always knew it and now everyone else does, too. Maura, although life hasn't always been kind to you, you have moved past those times of hurt and unfairness. You are a beautiful and intelligent young woman who has finally found her voice. Your strength amazes me. And lastly, to my husband John—you are my rock and have been for most of my life. Your love for me and belief in me truly touches my soul. —E. D.

ACRONYMS

ADD   attention deficit disorder

ADHD   attention deficit hyperactivity disorder

ASD   autism spectrum disorder

ASTART   Alliance for the Safe, Therapeutic & Appropriate Use of Residential Treatment

CBT   cognitive behavioral therapy

CARF   Commission on Accreditation of Rehabilitation Facilities

DAS-II   Differential Ability Scales

DSM   Diagnostic and Statistical Manual of Mental Disorders

DBT   dialectical behavioral therapy

EAL   equine-assisted learning

EAP   equine-assisted psychotherapy

EMDR   eye movement desensitization and reprocessing

IECA   Independent Educational Consultants Association

IEP   Individualized Education Program

JCAHO   Joint Commission on Accreditation of Healthcare Organizations (now the Joint Commission)

MDD	major depressive disorder
NATSAP	National Association of Therapeutic Schools and Programs
NATWC	National Association of Therapeutic Wilderness Camping
NIDA	National Institute on Drug Abuse
NLD	nonverbal learning disorder
OBHIC	Outdoor Behavioral Healthcare Industry Council
ODD	oppositional defiant disorder
PCT	person-centered therapy
PDD	pervasive developmental disorder
PPC	positive peer culture
PTSD	post-traumatic stress disorder
RTC	residential treatment center
SAD	separation anxiety disorder
SMART Recovery	Self Management and Recovery Training
TBS	therapeutic boarding school
TJC	The Joint Commission
T.R.A.I.L.S.	Therapeutic Riding Assists Individual Learning Skills
WAIS	Wechsler Adult Intelligence Scale
WISC-IV	Wechsler Intelligence Scale for Children
WJ III	Woodcock-Johnson Tests of Cognitive Abilities
WWASPS	World Wide Association of Specialty Programs and Schools

NOTES

[1] Ellen Behrens and Kristin Satterfield, "Longitudinal Family and Academic Outcomes in Residential Programs: How Students Function in Two Important Areas of Their Lives," *Journal of Therapeutic Schools and Programs* 2, no. 1 (2007): 81–94.

[2] Paul Case, *What Now?: How Teen Therapeutic Programs Could Save Your Troubled Child* (Franklin, TN: Common Thread Media, 2008), 41.

[3] Ibid., 61, 85. Italics ours.

[4] Frederic G. Reamer and Deborah H. Siegel, *Teens in Crisis: How the Industry Serving Struggling Teens Helps and Hurts Our Kids* (New York: Columbia University Press, 2008), 11–16.

[5] Ashley Wade (former counselor at Acadia Village (now called Village Behavioral Health), a residential treatment facility near Knoxville, Tennessee) in discussion with Rebecca Haid, (March 2010).

[6] Ellen Behrens and Kristin Satterfield, "A Multi-Center, Longitudinal Study of Youth Outcomes in Private Residential Treatment Facilities," (a paper presented at the Conference of the Independent Educational Consultants Association, Boston, April 27, 2007).

[7] Keith Russell, PhD, "Two Years Later: A Qualitative Assessment of Youth Well-Being and the Role of Aftercare in Outdoor Behavioral

Healthcare Treatment," *Child and Youth Care Forum* 34, no. 3 (2005): 209–39.

[8] "NATSAP Overview," last modified August 2, 2013, accessed August 14, 2013, http://natsap.org/about-natsap/overview/.

[9] "NATSAP Ethical Principles," last modified August 2, 2013, accessed August 14, 2013 http://natsap.org/principles-of-good-prac tice/ethical-principles/.

[10] Case, *What Now?,* 111.

[11] Case, *What Now?,* 92.

[12] David Dobbs, "Beautiful Brains," *National Geographic,* October 2011, http://ngm.nationalgeographic.com/2011/10/teenage-brains/ dobbs-text.

[13] John McKinnon, MD, foreword to *How Teen Therapeutic Programs Could Save Your Troubled Child* (Franklin, TN: Common Thread Media, 2007), 13.

[14] Reamer and Siegel, *Teens in Crisis,* 17.

[15] Liam Scheff, "Cedu Documentary Clip 5—Who Is Mel Wasser-man?" YouTube video, 9:38, excerpt from the documentary *Surviving Cedu,* February 10, 2009, www.youtube.com/watch?v=JXLfBbV2Xhg &feature=player_embedded.

[16] Ibid.

[17] *Wikipedia,* s.v. "Synanon," last modified June 24, 2013, http:// wikipedia.org/wiki/Synanon.

[18] Larry Stednitz, "Revisiting Mel Wasserman," Accountability Essays, *StrugglingTeens.com,* December 28, 2005, www.struggling teens.com/artman/publish/printer_5241.shtml.

[19] Liam Scheff, "Cedu Documentary Clip 5—Who Is Mel Wasser-man?" YouTube video, 9:38, excerpt from the documentary *Surviving Cedu,* February 10, 2009, www.youtube.com/watch?v=JXLfBbV2Xhg &feature=player_embedded.

[20] "The Birth of Outward Bound," accessed August 14, 2013, www. outwardbound.net/about-us/history/the-birth-of-outward-bound.

21 "Mission Statement," ANASAZI Foundation, accessed August 14, 2013, www.anasazi.org/mission.html.

22 Ibid.

23 Reamer and Siegel, *Teens in Crisis,* 115–16.

24 Ibid.

25 Ibid.

26 Case, *What Now?,* 25; Reamer and Siegel, *Teens in Crisis,* 108.

27 Reamer and Siegel, *Teens in Crisis,* 23.

28 Ibid., 79–80.

29 Spencer A. Rathus, *Psychology: Principles in Practice* (Austin: Hold, Rinehart, and Winston, 1998), 441–50.

30 Ibid., 548, 550.

31 Lisa Fritscher, "Therapeutic Milieu," last modified October 31, 2008, http://phobias.about.com/od/glossary/g/theramilieudef.htm.

32 William C. Wasmund, "Positive Peer Culture: Tapping an Invaluable Resource," *The International Child and Youth Care Network: CYC-Online* 110 (April 2008): www.cyc-net.org/cyc-online/cycol-0408-wasmund.html.

33 "Dr. Michael Clatch, Psy. D.," Courage to Connect Therapeutic Center, accessed July 2012, www.couragetoconnecttherapy.com/our-staff.

34 *Wikipedia,* s.v. "Person-centered therapy," last modified August 5, 2013, http://en.Wikipedia.org/wiki/Person-centered_therapy.

35 "What Is EAP and EAL?" Eagala, accessed July 20, 2012, www.eagala.org/Information/What_Is_EAP_EAL.

36 "Information," Eagala, accessed July 20, 2012, www.eagala.org/info.

37 "T.R.A.I.L.S," Reins to Recovery, Inc., accessed July 20, 2012, http://reinstorecovery.org/programs/t-r-a-i-l-s/.

38 "DrugFacts: Treatment Approaches for Drug Addiction," National Institute on Drug Abuse, last modified September 2009, accessed August 1, 2010, www.nida.nih.gov/Infofacts/TreatMeth.html.

[39] *Merriam-Webster Dictionary*, accessed September 17, 2013, http://www.merriam-webster.com/dictionary/12-step.

[40] "About Us," The Seven Challenges, accessed July 1, 2012, www.sevenchallenges.com/about.aspx.

[41] *Wikipedia*, s.v. "SMART Recovery," last modified June 25, 2013, http://en.wikipedia.org/wiki/SMART_Recovery.

[42] Jonathan Young, "Joseph Campbell's Mythic Journey," *New Perspectives* (July 1994): www.folkstory.com/campbell/campbell.html.

[43] Caryn L. Aman, "Methods and Philosophy," Full Circle, accessed July 1, 2012, www.carynaman.com/methods.aspx.

[44] *Wikipedia*, s.v. "Eye movement desensitization and reprocessing," last modified August 12, 2013, http://en.wikipedia.org/wiki/Eye_movement_desensitization_and_reprocessing.

[45] H. J. Hair, "Outcomes for Children and Adolescents After Residential Treatment: A Review of Research from 1993 to 2003," *Journal of Child and Family Studies* 14, no. 4 (December 2005), 551–75.

[46] Reggie Raman, MD, Parent's Orientation Workshop (Acadia Village (now called Village Behavioral Health) residential treatment center, Louisville, TN, October 5, 2009).

[47] Former academic advisor at Island View School, a residential treatment center near Salt Lake City, in discussion with Rebecca Haid (October 2009).

[48] Case, *What Now?*, 120.

[49] Ibid., 131–39.

[50] Reamer and Siegel, *Teens in Crisis*, 72.

[51] Ibid., 74.

[52] John Hechinger and Anne Marie Chaker, "Boarding School Options Shift for Troubled Teens," *Wall Street Journal*, March 31, 2005.

[53] Ibid.

[54] Reamer and Siegel, *Teens in Crisis*, 36.

[55] Margaret A. Keyes, PhD, Anu Sharma, PhD, Irene J. Elkins, PhD, William G. Iacono, PhD, and Matt McGue, PhD, "The Mental

Health of US Adolescents Adopted in Infancy," *Archives of Pediatrics & Adolescent Medicine* 162, no. 5 (May 2008): 419–25.

[56] Ibid.

[57] Evan B. Donaldson Adoption Institute, www.adoptioninstitute.org.

[58] M. T. Greenberg, "Attachment and Psychopathology in Childhood," in *Handbook of Attachment: Theory, Research, and Clinical Applications,* ed. J. Cassidy and P. R. Shaver (New York: Guilford Press, 1999), 469–96.

[59] Sara W. Lazar, George Bush, Randy L. Gollub, Gregory L. Fricchione, Gurucharan Khalsa, and Herbert Benson, "Functional Brain Mapping of the Relaxation Response and Meditation," *NeuroReport* 11, no. 715 (May 2000): 1581–85; Hans C. Lou, Troels W. Kjaer, Lars Friberg, Gordon Wildschiodtz, Søren Holm, Markus Nowak "A^{15}-H$_2$O PET Study of Meditation and the Resting State of Normal Consciousness," *Human Brain Mapping* 7, no. 2 (1999): 98–105; Andrew Newberg, Abass Alavi, Michael Baime, Michael Pourdehnad, Jill Santanna, and Eugene d'Aquili, "The Measurement of Regional Cerebral Blood Flow During the Complex Cognitive Task of Meditation: A Preliminary SPECT Study," *Psychiatry Research: Neuroimaging Section* 106 (2001): 113–22; Andrew Newberg, Michael Pourdehnad, Abass Alavi, and Eugene d'Aquili. "Cerebral Blood Flow during Meditative Prayer: Preliminary Findings and Methodological Issues,"*Pereceptual and Motor Skills* 97 (2003): 630–35.

[60] T. Wills, A. Yaeger, and J. Sandy, "Buffering Effects of Religiosity [*sic*] for Adolescent Substance Use," *Psychology of Addictive Behaviors* 13 (2003): 327–28; Shari Barkin, Shelley Kreiter, and Robert H. Durant, "Exposure to Violence and Intentions to Engage in Moralistic Violence During Early Adolescence," *Journal of Adolescence* 24, no. 6 (December 2001): 777–89; C. Lammers, M. Ireland, M. Resnick, and R. Blum, "Influences on Adolescents' Decision to Postpone Onset of Sexual Intercourse: A Survival Analysis of Virginity Among Youths Ages Thirteen to Eighteen Years," *Journal of Adolescent Health* 26 (2000): 42–48.

[61] *Wikipedia,* s.v. "Asperger syndrome," last modified August 15, 2013, http://en.wikipedia.org/wiki/Asperger_syndrome.

[62] *Wikipedia,* s.v. "Autism spectrum," last modified August 9, 2013, http://en.wikipedia.org/wiki/Autism_spectrum.

[63] "Borderline Personality Disorder," National Institutes of Mental Health, NIH Publication No. 11-4928, accessed April 30, 2013, www.nimh.nih.gov/health/publications/borderline-personality-disorder/what-is-borderline-personality-disorder.shtml.

[64] "Brainspotting™," David Grand, accessed April 30, 2013, www.brainspotting.pro.

[65] "Cognitive Behavioral Therapy (CBT)," National Alliance on Mental Illness, last modified July 2012, accessed April 20, 2013, www.nami.org/Template.cfm?Section=About_Treatments_and_Supports&Template=/ContentManagement/ContentDisplay.cfm&ContentID=141590.

[66] "DeEscalation," Crisis Intervention Team (CIT) International, accessed April 20, 2013, www.citinternational.org/training-overview/61-deescalation.html.

[67] "What Is EMDR?", Eye Movement Desensitization & Reprocessing Institute, accessed April 30, 2013, www.emdr.com/general-information/what-is-emdr.html.

[68] "Pervasive Development Disorders (PDDs)," WebMD, last modified May 12, 2013, accessed April 30, 2013, www.webmd.com/brain/autism/development-disorder.

[69] The Seven Challenges, accessed April 30, 2013, www.sevenchallenges.com.

GLOSSARY

504 Plans: Section 504 of the Federal Rehabilitation Act of 1973—For public school education, these plans provide for physical accommodations, such as wheelchair access, as well as provisions for materials, such as large-print textbooks or extended time on assignments or on tests.

After-care—A collaborative plan developed by therapeutic program professionals, parents, educational consultants, and other referring professionals to ensure that students have continued care once they return to the home environment. An after-care plan would identify local schools, therapists, support groups, and tutoring services to facilitate a smooth transition. Alternatively, after-care can be a proscribed plan that outlines next steps following wilderness.

Asperger's syndrome—an autism spectrum disorder (ASD) characterized by significant difficulties in social interaction, alongside restricted and repetitive patterns of behavior and interests. It differs from other autism spectrum disorders by its relative preservation of linguistic and cognitive development. Although not required for diagnosis, physical clumsiness and atypical (peculiar, odd) use of language are frequently reported.[61] With the new DSM-5, Asperger's syndrome is no longer considered a separate diagnosis, but is included under the auspices of autism spectrum disorder.

Autism spectrum disorder (ASD)—describes a range of conditions classified as pervasive developmental disorders (PDDs) in the DSM. These disorders are typically characterized by social deficits, communication difficulties, stereotyped or repetitive behaviors and interests, and in some cases, cognitive delays.[62]

Borderline personality disorder (BPD)—a serious mental illness marked by unstable moods, behavior, and relationships. Most people with BPD have problems with regulating emotions and thoughts, exhibit impulsive and reckless behavior, and have unstable relationships with other people. People with this disorder also have high rates of co-occurring disorders such as depression, anxiety disorders, substance abuse, and eating disorders, along with self-harm, suicidal behaviors, and completed suicides.[63]

Brainspotting—a powerful, focused treatment method that works by identifying, processing, and releasing core neurophysiological sources of emotional/body pain, trauma, dissociation, and a variety of challenging symptoms. Brainspotting was developed by Dr. David Grand in 2003 and identifies activated eye positions which correspond with the issue of disturbance.[64]

Cognitive behavioral therapy (CBT)—a form of treatment that focuses on examining the relationships between thoughts, feelings, and behaviors. By exploring patterns of thinking that lead to self-destructive actions and the beliefs that direct these thoughts, people with mental illness can modify their patterns of thinking to improve coping. With CBT, the therapist and the patient will actively work together to help the patient recover from his or her mental illness.[65]

Dialectical behavioral therapy (DBT)—a specialized form of cognitive behavioral therapy developed by Dr. Marsha Linehan and her colleagues at the University of Washington. DBT incorporates a client evaluation of his or her own distortions of thought along with the implementation of meditation and mindfulness, with the overall goal of reducing anxiety and providing the client with a skill set to use in coping with and diffusing maladaptive, destructive thoughts and behaviors.

De-escalation techniques—mental health professionals, program staff, and transport teams utilize these techniques to lower stress-related behaviors exhibited by clients presented with circumstances they feel are beyond their control. Techniques include nonverbal de-escalation, such as appearing calm, maintaining eye contact, and keeping a relaxed posture, and verbal de-escalation, such as keeping a low-modulated voice tone and showing honesty, respect, and empathy for the particular situation.[66]

Diagnostic and Statistical Manual of Mental Disorders (DSM) — published by the American Psychiatric Association, the DSM provides a common language for diagnosis of mental disorders. The DSM-5, a greatly revised version, was published May 18, 2013.

Executive functions—a set of mental functions that control how a person connects past experience with current situations, plans and organizes tasks, manages time and attention, remembers details, inhibits actions, sets goals, and follows through with those goals.

Eye movement desensitization and reprocessing (EMDR)—a psychotherapy that enables people to heal from the symptoms and emotional distress that are the result of disturbing life experiences. EMDR therapy shows that the mind can in fact heal from psychological trauma, much as the body recovers from physical trauma.[67]

Emotional-growth schools—characterized by a structured and supportive therapeutic curriculum. The emphasis is on moral growth and development by giving students autonomy to make informed choices.

Equine therapy—the discipline of using horses as a means to provide metaphoric experiences in order to promote emotional growth.

Individualized Education Program (IEP)—formal written plans and program strategies for students who meet the federal requirements for special education. Mandated under the Individuals with Disabilities Education Improvement Act of 2004 (IDEA 2004), the IEP prescribes educational goals and outlines the methods by which students will try to meet those goals. Every student who qualifies for an IEP has a document tailored for his or her unique needs, and the plan is updated on a regular basis until the student has graduated from high school or until he or she reaches the age of twenty-two.

Milieu therapy—focuses on the interactions of people within a particular community to effect individual change. In therapeutic residential programs, the community comprises students as well as staff and emphasizes the importance of community roles and responsibilities.

Neuropsychological evaluation—an assessment tool through which in-depth information is obtained about a student's cognitive, motor, behavioral, linguistic, and executive functioning.

Person-centered therapy or Rogerian therapy—focuses on creating a safe, nonjudgmental environment for students by consistently providing empathy and unconditional positive regard for them during a therapeutic session. The goal is to help students find their own solutions to problems and destructive behaviors.

Pervasive developmental disorder (PDD)—refers to a group of conditions that involve delays in the development of many basic skills, most notably the ability to socialize with others, to communicate, and to use imagination. Children with these conditions are often confused in their thinking and generally have problems understanding the world around them. Autism, Asperger's syndrome, and pervasive developmental disorder not otherwise specified (PDD-NOS) are classified as pervasive developmental disorders.[68]

Positive peer culture (PPC)—a therapeutic approach that focuses on the interactions, group discussions, and constructive feedback to effect change within a particular peer community. The PPC approach posits that students are more likely to internalize change when held accountable by their peers rather than the adults responsible for their care.

Psychoeducational evaluation—a group of tests used to assess aptitude, academic achievement, and social/emotional and personality functioning. Common tests include: Wechsler Intelligence Scale for Children® (WISC-IV), Wechsler Adult Intelligence Scale (WAIS), Differential Ability Scales—Second Edition (DAS-II), and Woodcock-Johnson Tests of Cognitive Abilities (WJ III).

Rehab—a term usually used to describe drug or alcohol rehabilitation. Rehab programs are usually short-term interventional programs that last from thirty to forty-five days. Rehab can include an initial in-patient stay at a detoxification facility to gain medical stabilization.

Residential treatment center (RTC)—clinically intensive, closely supervised, and highly structured therapeutic environments. RTCs can range from in-patient, hospital-based facilities to intimate programs that replicate homelike environments. Common diagnoses of students who are referred to RTCs include those who have experienced sexual trauma, post-traumatic stress disorder (PTSD), attempted suicide, suicidal ideation, psychosis, conduct disorders, and mood disorders. Short-term programs for complex neuropsychological and behavioral assessments are also included in this classification.

Seven Challenges model—an evidence-based program designed specifically for adolescents with drug problems intended to motivate a decision and commitment to change and to support success in implementing the desired changes. The challenges provide a framework for helping youth think through their own decisions about their lives and their use of alcohol and other drugs.[69]

SMART Recovery (Self Management and Recovery Training)—an addiction model that is sometimes used as an alternative to the Twelve Steps. SMART Recovery combines therapeutic techniques from motivational enhancement therapy and cognitive behavioral therapy. The program focuses on four major points in the recovery process: building the student's motivation, helping them cope with urges, enhancing problem solving, and balancing lifestyle choices.

Therapeutic boarding school (TBS)—a therapeutic residential program that is considered to be a mid-level option on the continuum between an RTC and an emotional-growth school. A TBS often provides a balance among therapeutic intervention, academic achievement, and social/emotional growth. A typical length of stay for a TBS is twelve to eighteen months.

Transport services—companies hired to accompany students to their schools or programs. Individual employees often have backgrounds in private investigation, law enforcement, mental health, or a combination thereof.

Twelve-Step model for addiction—a set of guidelines that emphasizes a person's need to admit that he or she cannot control the addiction or compulsion and recognize that a higher, spiritual power is needed to overcome the problem. Additionally, the recovering addict must examine the past mistakes they've made with the help of an experienced sponsor and try to make amends. The recovering addict then begins to live a new life with a new code of behavior and strives to help others who are suffering from the same addictions or compulsions.

Wilderness—a short-term interventional program usually set in remote areas away from the distractions of popular culture. Emphasis is on clean living, learning accountability for past destructive actions, and learning to live in community. Backcountry adventure activities such as hiking, climbing, or canyoneering are typical components of the experiential curriculum. Wilderness is intended to be a first step in the recovery process and is generally followed by a referral to a residential therapeutic program.

Young adult programs or "over eighteens"—for students over the age of eighteen who are facing a difficult transition to adulthood, young adult programs are most beneficial to ensure success on the path to independent living. Young adult transition programs provide support—social/emotional, behavioral, and academic—to build confidence and a strong foundation necessary for the health and well-being of their adult students.

RESOURCES

Publications

Teens in Crisis: How the Industry Serving Struggling Teens Helps and Hurts Our Kids by Frederic G. Reamer and Deborah Siegel (Columbia University Press, 2008)

An outstanding overview of the therapeutic boarding school industry. *Teens in Crisis* takes a balanced look at the pros and cons of considering residential programs. Although it is written primarily for an academic audience, it provides invaluable information for parents as well.

To Change a Mind: Parenting to Promote Maturity in Teenagers by John A. McKinnon, MD (Lantern Books, 2010)

Psychiatrist John McKinnon, the founder of Montana Academy, provides insight on effective parenting techniques.

An Unchanged Mind: The Problem of Immaturity in Adolescence by John A. McKinnon, MD (Lantern Books, 2008)

McKinnon explores the underlying causes of trouble with struggling teenagers and explains his decision to found a therapeutic boarding school.

What It Takes to Pull Me Through: Why Teenagers Get in Trouble and How Four of Them Got Out by David L. Marcus (Mariner Books, 2006)

This book profiles several struggling teenagers and the different paths they took toward healing and stability.

What Now?: How Teen Therapeutic Programs Could Save Your Troubled Child by Dr. Paul Case (Common Thread Media, 2008)

One of the clinical directors of Open Sky Wilderness explains the therapeutic process for children enrolled in emotional-growth and therapeutic schools and what parents can expect along the way.

Online

The Campbell Collaboration (www.campbellcollaboration.org) and the Cochrane Reviews (www.cochrane.org/cochrane-reviews)

Both these publications offer constantly updated information on the best mental health care modalities available based on the most current research. Although written primarily for professional clinicians, they are accessible and clear reports for parents as well.

The Independent Educational Consultants Association (www.iecaonline.com)

The IECA provides up-to-date referral information for educational consultants, average costs, and a general overview of the services provided by members and the association.

The National Association of Therapeutic Schools and Programs (www.natsap.org)

NATSAP provides an updated list of all their affiliated schools and programs along with a description of the different services provided by these facilities.

Open Sky Wilderness Therapy (www.openskywildnerness.com)

Open Sky, one of the largest wilderness education programs in the country, provides information on their staff, program locations, and goals through this website.

Second Nature Therapeutic Wilderness Programs (www.snwp.com)

Second Nature is another well-known, widely respected wilderness therapy provider. Their website has information on programs, locations, staff backgrounds, and their overall mission.

Woodbury Reports, Inc. (www.strugglingteens.com)

Educational consultant Lon Woodbury compiles IECA member reports and comments on the various therapeutic schools and programs they've visited, giving consultants and parents alike an updated overview of developments in the field.

ABOUT THE AUTHORS

REBECCA HAID received her master's degree in speech pathology and audiology from the University of Georgia in 1983. A longtime mental health advocate, she served for nearly a decade on the board of directors for The Link, a not-for-profit counseling and mental health facility in Atlanta. Rebecca is also  the author of *Waiting for Answers: A Parent's Guide to Grief, Resolution, and Healing.* She and her husband, Reg, currently live in Atlanta.

ELIZABETH W. DONNELLY holds a BA from the University of Virginia in German language and literature and a MS in educational psychology from Georgia State University. She is a professional member of the Independent Educational Consultants Association (IECA) and an affiliate member of  the National Association of Therapeutic Schools and Programs (NATSAP). Elizabeth remains committed to the education and support of youth not only professionally but also in her personal life and in the local community as well. She lives in Atlanta with her husband, John.

ABOUT THE PUBLISHER

LANTERN BOOKS was founded in 1999 on the principle of living with a greater depth and commitment to the preservation of the natural world. In addition to publishing books on animal advocacy, vegetarianism, religion, and environmentalism, Lantern is dedicated to printing books in the United States on recycled paper and saving resources in day-to-day operations. Lantern is honored to be a recipient of the highest standard in environmentally responsible publishing from the Green Press Initiative.

www.lanternbooks.com